MAKE YOUR OWN MUSIC VIDEO

JAMES B. MEIGS AND
JENNIFER STERN

FRANKLIN WATTS
NEW YORK I LONDON I TORONTO
SYDNEY I 1986
A FIRST BOOK

DIAGRAMS BY ANNE CANEVARI GREEN

Photographs courtesy of: Atlantic Records: p. 13; Gary
Gershoff: p. 21; Sony Corporation: p. 25; Ambico: p. 26
(left); Bilora: p. 26 (right); Zenith Electronics Corporation:
p. 27 (top); JVC: p. 27 (bottom); the authors: pp. 44, 56;
© 1985 MCA Videocassette Inc.: p. 51; Just Loomis: p. 66.

Library of Congress Cataloging in Publication Data
Meigs, James B.
Make your own music video.

(A First book)
Bibliography: p.
Includes index.
Summary: Explains the capabilities of videotape equipment
and guides the beginner through planning, writing,
shooting, editing, and distributing a music video.
1. Music videos—Production and direction—Juvenile
literature. [1. Music videos—Production and direction.
2. Video recording—Production and direction]
I. Stern, Jennifer A. II. Title.
PN1992.8.M87M45 1986   784.5   86-9077
ISBN 0-531-10215-7

CONTENTS

THE AUTHORS GIVE SPECIAL THANKS TO
ROCK PERFORMER LOUIS MULKERN, TO
AMBICO, N.A.P. CONSUMER ELECTRONICS
AND OLYMPUS AND TO
ANDREA RUSKIN AND KEN WALZ
FOR THEIR HELP IN WRITING THIS BOOK.

1 WHAT IS MUSIC VIDEO?

Your favorite rock star struts and sings right in the middle of your living room. In front of the band, thousands of cheering fans sway to the music. Suddenly, the scene changes, and you see the lead singer running across a desert, still singing the same song. What's happening here? It's a music *video*, and you're watching it on TV.

Just a few years ago, there was no such thing as music video on TV. Instead, people heard music groups on the radio. They never knew whether their favorite singer was fat or thin, black or white, tall or short, unless they happened to see a picture in a music magazine or on an album cover, or saw the performer in a concert on TV or live. But in 1981, the cable TV channel *MTV* (Music Television) came along and changed everything. Today, when we decide whether or not we like a band or a singer, how they look and how they dance is just as important as how the music sounds.

We can now see music video all day long on MTV. We can also see it on regular broadcast TV channels on programs like *Friday Night Videos*. However, though it's new to TV, music video is not really new at all. It's been around a long time, but in different forms.

Music video is, basically, moving pictures put to music. Music and moving pictures have gone together ever since the first *talkie* movie, *The Jazz Singer,* was made in 1927. More recently, rock bands such as the Beatles have made movies and there have been movie musicals like *Flashdance.* There have also been TV shows like *American Bandstand*, where rock and roll stars of the sixties, seventies, and eighties performed their songs. And sometimes, rock and roll groups like the Rolling Stones would get together to make music videos without really knowing who would ever see them. After all, there were no music video TV programs around on which to air them.

Today's music stars have many different ways to show their videos to the general public. Besides MTV and various TV programs on *broadcast* and *cable TV*, there are movie theaters where videos are sometimes shown before the main movie. There is also home video. More and more families today have *video cassette recorders (VCRs,* for short) or *video disc players.* Music videos are found on tapes or discs that can be bought or rented at any video store.

There are many different kinds of music videos. The simplest are *performance videos.* For these, the music video producers, using one or two or more cameras and sound-recording equipment, record an actual concert.

Conceptual videos are more complex. We see conceptual videos on TV more often than performance videos. ''Conceptual'' comes from the word ''concept,'' which means ''idea.'' These are videos based on an idea or a story. In conceptual videos, the musicians do not just perform their music. They become actors, playing parts in fictional situations. Sometimes a singer will pretend to be in love with another performer and will sing a love song to him or her. Sometimes the musicians will dress up as bus drivers or waitresses or cowboys or teachers. The part they play relates to the song they sing. For instance, a bus driver might sing, ''I love to drive those four-lane highways.''

Some conceptual videos don't show any people at all. Some, for example, just show animated shapes moving around the screen in time to the music. Other conceptual videos mix some shots of the group performing with the shots of them acting.

In many conceptual videos, the performers look like they're singing the song, but they're not. These videos use a technique called *lip-synching*. This means that the performer moves his or her lips *synchronously* (in time) with music that has already been recorded. It's not always easy to tell if lip-synching has been used in a video, but when you see and hear a performer singing softly in the middle of a howling wind storm, you know the voice couldn't possibly have been recorded at the same time the picture was.

Most videos made today are quite short. They usually last only as long as a song does—about three to five minutes. Today, musicians and video directors are also experimenting with *long-form videos*. These videos are often half an hour long. Some consist of lots of talking and a song or two. Others feature one song that goes on and on, and others, many songs strung together.

We use the word "video" to refer to the music clips we see on TV. But video has another meaning, too. It refers to one of two methods used to record moving pictures. The other method is *film*.

Video is used to make the pictures you see on your television set. The pictures you get from your antenna or from the cable company and the pictures you get from your video cassette recorder or video disc player are all video pictures.

Film is used to make the moving pictures you watch in a movie theater. It is also used to make still photographs.

Both video and film use cameras to make pictures. Both also make moving pictures by taking many still pictures in a row. These still pictures are called *frames*. *Film cameras* take twenty-four frames a second, and *video cameras* take thirty frames a second. When the finished movies are played that fast, you can't tell that separate pictures were taken at all.

Video and film both use frames, but they make those frames in very different ways. In video, each frame is made a little at a time. Each frame is made of thousands of tiny dots, like a newspaper picture or a needlepoint picture. These dots are called *picture elements*.

When your TV plays a frame, it puts these dots onto the screen one at a time in the same way you put down letters on a piece of paper when you write.

In film, a frame is not made up of many different parts. Each frame is made all at once. When you see a film movie, each frame is played all at once.

Film is a material containing chemicals that are sensitive to light. If you hold up a piece of film to a picture of a white dot against a black background, the chemicals will change where the white dot is. When the film is developed, it's treated with other chemicals that make this change visible.

Each frame of film is a picture made exactly this way. Each is made by exposing a little piece of a long strip of film running through the camera to the light bouncing off the people and things the camera is pointed at. A picture of those people and things is recorded on the film by the chemicals. Each second, twenty-four little pieces of film are exposed.

Most professional music-video makers shoot their clips on film and then transfer them to video to play on TV. They believe the colors and other details of the picture come out better when the videos are made that way.

Making a professional music video is, of course, a lot more complicated and more expensive than making one at home. But to give you a good idea of how a professional music-video *shoot* is done, let's take a look at how one professional video was made.

The Beatles were one of the first rock bands to combine their songs with moving pictures. This is a scene from their hit movie Help!

2
HOW THE PROS DO IT

It's long after midnight, but a large crew is still hard at work shooting the final scenes of Raven's "On and On" rock video. "Won't take your fooling around," sings Raven's lead singer John Gallagher, as he leaps from the floodlit stage. Fans rock to the thunderous music.

To many people, this might seem like a scene from one of the British heavy-metal group's concerts. But anyone who looks closely will see that the band members aren't really playing. Their instruments aren't even plugged in! The music is a tape of Raven's "On and On" single played through powerful speakers. The band is only mouthing the words in time to the music and pretending to play. But it looks good to the camera, and that's what counts.

*The members of the rock band Raven are
John Gallagher (left), Mark Gallagher
(right), and drummer Wacko.*

The band and crew have been working on this video since early this morning, but the preparation began weeks ago.

PLANNING THE VIDEO

It all started when Atlantic Records, the company that puts out Raven's records, decided to produce a video to promote the band's new album. Almost all the video clips seen on TV are produced for the same reason: the record company hopes that people will like the video and will want to buy the record. In this way, music video clips are a lot like commercials. In fact, many of the most famous music video directors, like Bob Giraldi, who shot Michael Jackson's "Beat It" clip, also make commercials.

Atlantic decided to spend fifty thousand dollars on the Raven video. This is enough money to buy a small house in many parts of the country. However, most of the videos on TV cost even more. Michael Jackson's "Thriller" video, for example, cost about one million dollars. It was one of the most expensive ever made.

Next, the record company chose a producer, Ken Walz. Ever since he produced Cyndi Lauper's first hit video, "Girls Just Wanna Have Fun," Walz has been one of the most famous music video producers. He chose a director for the clip Amos Poe, who had directed such movies as *Alphabet City*.

The jobs of producer and director are very different. The *producer* is in charge of making all the arrangements for the shoot: renting the equipment, hiring the crew, getting permission to shoot in all the necessary locations, and checking many other details. All this planning occurs during the *preproduction* stage of the video. It's called preproduction because it happens before any of the actual shooting takes place. In fact, according to Walz, "The day of the shoot, the producer is the only one who doesn't have anything to do." He or she stands around to make sure all the arrangements made beforehand are working out.

The job of the *director* is to make sure everything looks good in the video. He or she encourages the band and actors to perform well and tries to make every scene exciting to watch.

Even though there aren't usually any spoken words in a music video, somebody still has to write a script for it. (The only videos that don't have scripts are the ones that are shot during an actual concert.) Poe wrote the script for "On and On." To write it, he first had to think of a concept for the video. His idea was to show the band, dressed up as poor boys, begging different record companies to hire them to make a record.

Walz made sure that the finished script contained no scenes that would be too expensive to shoot. For example, there couldn't be one scene on a street in New York and another on the beach in Florida. It would cost too much to fly the band and crew back and forth. Because of the small budget, the video had to be shot all in one place and all in one day.

After the script was finished, Walz showed it to the record company. The company liked it and suggested only a few changes. You can see part of the script on pages 16-17. It describes every single camera shot in the video, as well as every action the band and other actors would make.

Once Atlantic approved the script, Walz and his assistant, Andrea Ruskin, started making arrangements for the actual shoot. They lined up a studio to shoot in, a warehouselike building that had once been a roller-skating rink, in New York's Staten Island. They hired all the crew members and rented all the equipment. They even made sure everyone—cast and crew—would have enough to eat.

THE SHOOT

Finally, it was time for the shoot. The day's schedule, made up by Ruskin, lists the order in which every scene in the video is to be shot. The scenes are not shot in the same order they appear in in the finished clip, but rather in the order that's most convenient. The Raven video was shot on film, like most professional videos.

"ON AND ON"*

Artist: RAVEN
Client: Atlantic Records
Producer: Ken Walz
Writer/Director: Amos Poe

9. Intro	In the dilapidated office of "Rusty Records," a funny looking little bald guy, wearing a white shirt, tie, green visor and glasses, is sitting at a large desk listening to the song on a Walkman. John, Wacko, and Mark are standing in front of him, dressed like poor boys from a Dickens story.
10. Intro	Close-up of little guy's face as he listens on headphones, and obviously disapproving of the music.
11. Intro	Close-ups of our lads as they look forlornly at each other.
12. Intro	Wide shot as the little guy's secretary shows the boys out of the office.
13. Intro	Close-up of the little guy looking over his bifocals.
14. Intro	Cut to the lads lounging in their dingy quarters.
15. Can't take the pace	Camera suspended from a rope in center of room, spins manically.
16. It gets me riled	Close-up with extreme wide angle of JG singing.

17. First you say	Raven in the office of "Greedy Records." Everything is the same except name of company: same secretary and little guy.
18. No	Close-up of little guy shaking his head.
19. Then you drive me wild	Medium shot of the secretary, standing by the door as she adjusts her reading glasses.
20. Ain't gonna take it anymore	Gallagher moves up in front of the little guy and sings into his face.
21. Bolt the windows	Three close-ups of windows slamming in rapid succession.
22. Lock your door	Extra close-up of key locking a door.
23. You're gonna see what I've got in store	Wacko, JG, and MG surround the secretary, as JG sings to her, his nose almost touching hers in a mock threat.
24. You're gonna get what's coming to you right now	J, W, and M singing to the little guy, scaring him half to death, so that he jumps into the secretary's arms. She holds him. (Close-up, then wide shot.) FREEZE
25. It goes on and on and on and on and on	The lads jump through the frozen image (CK) and are out in the hall, followed by a dozen white-collar workers who are singing along.
26. Won't take your fooling around	The lads walking towards the camera, and JG pointing into camera as he walks.

*Shots 9 through 26 excerpted from actual script.

On the big day, everyone shows up very early. The crew members, more than twenty of them, get straight to work setting up the first scene.

Different members of the crew have different jobs. The *cameraperson* is responsible for running the camera, following the director's recommendations. He or she may also give the director advice on how a certain shot might look better. The cameraperson also has a helper, the *assistant camera,* who helps carry around the equipment, changes the film in the camera, and sometimes even helps focus the camera. The person in charge of setting up the lights is the *gaffer.* (The gaffer had several helpers on the Raven shoot.) The *sound person* operates a large tape recorder that's used to play the song during every shot. A number of *production assistants* are there to pitch in whenever they're needed. PAs, as they're called, might do anything from moving furniture to painting a wall to running out to buy a light bulb if one burns out.

The first scene on the schedule is to take place in an office. By eight in the morning, the PAs are hard at work turning a corner of the huge empty studio into something that will look like an office on the TV screen. First, they make some scenery that looks like a wall with a window in it. Then they paint the walls. They move a desk and chairs into position and hang a sign saying Rusty Records on the wall.

The gaffer sets up several different kinds of lights, some pointing at the desk, some at the walls, some at the ceiling. He tries to re-create in the studio the kind of light you'd find in a real office, then adds even more to make sure the actors' faces show up when they're on TV.

The cameraperson and his assistant move the camera into position and check how the scene looks through the camera's *viewfinder.* The director keeps his eye on all of this, making small changes in the positions of lights and furniture.

Meanwhile, Raven band members John and Mark Gallagher and Wacko are getting dressed in their "poor boy" outfits, and two actors hired to appear in the video get into their costumes and make-up. Poe, the director, calls all of them onto the set for a rehearsal. The actor described in the script as "the little guy" sits behind the desk. His "secretary" sits by the desk, and the three band members stand in front of them. The director coaches them on what to do during the scene. The little guy is a record company executive. In this scene, Raven is supposed to be begging him to hire them and put out their record.

"Playback," shouts the director. The sound person punches a button on the tape recorder, and the opening notes of "On and On" boom through the studio. John, Mark, and Wacko nod to the music while the little guy pretends to listen on headphones. He shakes his head disapprovingly. "Cut!" yells the director, and the music dies. Though the whole scene took only a few seconds, the director has quite a few pointers for the band and actors. "Instead of just nodding your head, Wacko, why don't you pound the desk with your hand, too?" he says. After a few more rehearsals, they're ready to shoot the scene for real.

"Playback," the director yells again. The music booms. "Rolling!" says the cameraperson as he turns on the camera. "Action!" The little guy listens and shakes his head, and John, Mark, and Wacko nod along as the first few seconds of the song roll by. "Cut!" the director yells. "That was really good," he tells the band, "but let's try it again with more movement. Really move to the music."

It takes three more tries, but they finally get it right. Now it's time to shoot the same scene again, only this time with close-ups of the little guy and the band members' faces as they watch him unhappily. When the video is pieced together afterward, these close-ups will be mixed in with the other shots.

These shots also take several tries to get right. The director keeps yelling "Cut!" There's always a different reason why everything has to stop: the makeup person has to touch up someone's makeup, one of the lights is casting a harsh shadow and has to be moved, the camera runs out of film. Shooting a rock video takes a lot of patience.

Shooting the rest of the office scenes takes until lunchtime. By now the shoot is two hours behind schedule.

More scenes follow in the long afternoon. Almost every shot has to be done more than once. The cameraperson saves all the film he shoots, even scenes he or the director thinks didn't work out right. After the film is developed, the producer and director will want to look over all the shots before choosing which ones to put in the video clip.

By nightfall, everyone has been working for almost twelve hours, but some of the most important scenes still have to be shot. A number of the band's helpers (known as "roadies" in the music business) are putting the finishing touches on the dramatic set Raven uses in its live performances.

Early in the evening, the crowd in the studio suddenly grows more numerous when a large group of extras troops in. An *extra* is anyone who appears in a video, TV show, or movie in a tiny part. These extras play the part of fans cheering on the band in the final scenes of the "On and On" clip. Since Raven is a heavy-metal band, the extras are dressed for the part: they wear enough black leather to clothe a motorcycle gang.

Even though most of the people in the studio are still hard at work, the shoot is beginning to seem like a party. Friends and people from the record company drop in to see how the shoot is going. MTV VJ (video jockey) Nina Blackwood comes to get an advance look at a clip she knows she'll be playing on MTV in a few weeks.

The crew is finally ready to shoot the final "performance" scene in the early hours of the morning. Raven climbs on stage and rocks through the final lines of "On and On." The extras cheer with excitement. They're not just actors and actresses, they're real Raven fans and they're enjoying the chance to be in a Raven video.

The cameraman moves in for a close-up
of John Gallagher during the shooting
of Raven's "On and On" video.

By the next morning, the lights, cameras, and other equipment will be gone. All the sets, including the "office" and even the large concert set, will be torn down. The huge studio will be as bare and empty as it was before the shooting began.

POSTPRODUCTION

Although the shooting is over, the work for Walz and Poe is only half done. The phase called *production* is finished. Now it's time to start *postproduction.*

The most important part of postproduction is *editing.* Editing is the process of putting the video together from the many rolls of film shot during the production day. Walz and Poe will select the very best shots and then arrange them in the order described in the script.

After the film has been developed, Walz and Poe sit down with an editor, whose job is helping producers and directors to put the bits and pieces of their video together. Using a miniature projector called an "editing table," they look at all of the film and choose the best versions, or "takes," of each scene. They cut out these best shots and then reattach, or *splice,* them together. There are hundreds of separate pieces of film to keep in order and to piece together. When the editing is finished, the film footage is converted into video tape footage at a *video facility,* a company whose equipment includes a machine that plays back the film and records all the images on video tape.

Although Walz and Poe edited their video when it was in film form, most producers have all the film shot during production transferred to video tape and *then* edit it. Sitting at a control panel, which looks almost like the flight deck of a spaceship and has buttons to control several video tape recorders and a number of TV screens, they choose the footage they like by watching it on the screens. The chosen shots are transferred one by one from the original video tape to a blank tape on another video tape recorder. These producers and editors never touch the tape itself. The video image is simply shifted electronically from one recorder to the other.

After the video is in its final form on video tape, the sound is finally added. The process of adding sound to the video tape is called *dubbing,* from the word "double." The soundtrack that ends up on the video tape is a double of the sound recorded on the original audio tape. The sound and the pictures fit together perfectly because of the computerized editing system at the video facility. When Walz and the editor see Wacko bring his drumstick down hard on the cymbal, they hear a crash in the middle of the song.

After weeks of work, Walz finally sees the completed Raven video just as it will appear on TV in a few weeks.

After the record company approves the finished version, the video facility makes copies of it. The company then sends them to MTV, *Friday Night Videos,* and any other music video shows they want to play it. Within a few days, "On and On," which started as a few ideas on a piece of paper, is on TV screens all over the country.

3 YOUR EQUIPMENT: WHAT YOU NEED AND HOW IT WORKS

Like the professionals, you have a choice of making your music clip with video or film equipment. Because you can rent or borrow any equipment you need to make your clip, you should base your decision on what equipment you have available to play the clip back. After all, you want to be able to watch the finished clip any time you want. So, if you or any of your friends has a video cassette recorder at home, use video equipment. If you don't, but you do have a film projector, then film might be a better choice.

VIDEO EQUIPMENT

What equipment will you need for a video shoot? You can use either a video camera and a portable VCR or a *camcorder,* which is a combination camera–video recorder. Most large video stores today rent this equipment. You can get a video camera and a portable VCR for fifty dollars to a hundred dollars a day or a camcorder for about the same price.

(24)

*Sony's tiny Handycam (above) is the smallest
8-mm video camcorder. It records pictures and
sound on the 8-mm videocassette pictured next
to it. The Video 8 playback deck (below) plays
the pictures back on a TV set.*

Above: Powerful movie lights such as this one help illuminate the action in music videos. This light has special flaps, called barn doors, *to help aim the light where it's needed. Right: a tripod is a three-legged stand for a camera. It helps hold the camera steady during shooting.*

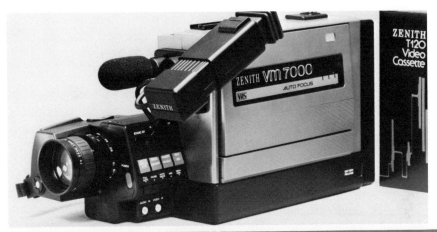

Above: VHS camcorders such as this one can record pictures and sound on full-size VHS videocassettes just like those used in tabletop VHS VCRs. Below: a VHS tabletop video cassette recorder is the most common type of video equipment in homes. You can use it to play back your music video or, if it's connected to a video camera, to shoot a video.

People under the age of eighteen can't rent equipment without a parent and, usually, a credit card, so make sure you bring a parent along. Once you have the equipment, be sure to be very careful with it. As the expression goes, "You break it, you buy it!"

THE VIDEO CASSETTE RECORDER

A video cassette recorder (VCR) is the most common and most basic kind of video equipment. It's what you'll use to play back your music clip when it's finished. Today, many families have VCRs in their homes. Most use them for taping shows on TV so they can watch them later. Many families also use VCRs to watch movies they rent or buy at the video store. For these purposes, most families have *tabletop VCRs.* They're called tabletop VCRs because they are too large and heavy to do anything except sit on top of a table.

There is a second kind of VCR that can do the same things a tabletop VCR can do, and more. It's called a *portable VCR,* because it's light enough to carry around. Portable VCRs are actually tabletop VCRs that can split in half. One half, the *tuner/timer,* tunes in the TV programs. Since it's not needed for making home movies, it can be left behind. The other half, which does the recording, goes with you when you make your video. You can carry it on your shoulder using a strap. This half also has batteries so you don't have to worry about finding an electrical outlet for a cord.

To make a home video movie with a portable VCR, you also need a video camera. You attach the camera to the portable VCR with a long cable. The camera works with the VCR in the same way your eye works with your brain. The camera "sees" the scene and converts it into video signals that the VCR can understand. The VCR "remembers" the scene by recording it on video tape.

Although all video cameras speak in the same signal language, a language that all VCRs can understand, all cameras cannot be used with all portable VCRs. Cameras and portable VCRs use different camera-to-VCR plugs. When you choose a camera to use with your portable VCR, pick one that's the same brand as your VCR. If that's not possible, ask the people at the video store what other cameras you could use.

Instead of using a portable VCR and camera to make your movie, you can use a camcorder. A camcorder does the job of a camera and a portable VCR. Camcorders are usually easier to use for beginners. You can rent them, too.

All VCRs and camcorders use a video cassette, with video tape inside it, to record video pictures and sound. However, different VCRs and camcorders use different-size cassettes. There are four different sizes of cassettes today: VHS, VHS-C, Beta, and 8 mm (millimeter). These sizes are called *formats.*

VHS cassettes are the largest. They're about the size of a paperback book. VHS cassettes use tape .5 inch (1.3 cm) wide. They can only be played on VHS VCRs.

VHS-C cassettes are relatives of VHS cassettes. They are much smaller than VHS cassettes, but they also use .5-inch tape. Because they are smaller, VHS-C portable VCRs and camcorders are much lighter than VHS portables and camcorders. However, VHS-C is used only for movie making. There are no tabletop VHS-C VCRs. You can, however, play back a VHS-C tape on a VHS tabletop VCR by using a special adapter the size of a VHS cassette.

Beta cassettes are bigger than VHS-C cassettes, but smaller than VHS cassettes. They use .5-inch tape and can only be played back on Beta VCRs.

The *8-mm* cassettes are the smallest. They use tape that's 8-mm wide, approximately .3 inch (.8 cm). You can only play back 8-mm tapes on an 8-mm VCR or camcorder.

Unlike *audio cassette* recorders, VCRs can run at different speeds. (Few camcorders can do this.) In VHS, SP (which stands for "standard play") is the fastest, LP ("long play") is slower, and EP ("extended play") is the slowest. In Beta, Beta II is usually the fastest and Beta III is the slowest. (Older home Beta VCRs and some professional Beta VCRs have a very fast Beta I speed, but it's not used on any modern home VCRs.) In 8-mm, there is an SP speed and an

LP speed. Not all VCRs record and play in all the speeds. Camcorders record only in the fastest speed.

The slower the speed you use, the more playing time you can get on each cassette. However, we recommend that you use the *fastest* speed your VCR has for shooting your video. Why? Well, first of all, you won't need a lot of playing time to make a music video. And second, you'll get a better picture at the fastest speed. At the fastest speed, the VCR uses more tape to make each picture. More tape means more information can be recorded about each picture. And more information means a better picture. So, if you're using a VHS VCR, do your shooting in SP. If you're using a Beta recorder, shoot in Beta II or Beta I. And with 8-mm, use SP.

There are also some VHS and Beta VCRs that can give you better sound to go with your picture. These are called *Hi-Fi* VCRs. Usually, in VHS and Beta, sound is recorded on a tiny strip along the edge of the .5-inch video tape. Because this strip is so narrow, the sound quality it produces is not very good. (Remember, more tape means more information.) In Hi-Fi VCRs, the sound information, like the picture information, is recorded across the whole width of the video tape, resulting in sound quality better than a record or an audio cassette. Hi-Fi VCRs also record sound along the narrow strip at the edge of the tape so that any tape made on a Hi-Fi VCR can be played on a non–Hi-Fi VCR—and vice versa.

Unfortunately, this Hi-Fi process poses a problem for music video makers. Because the Hi-Fi sound is recorded *along with the picture,* rather than on a separate strip, you can't add Hi-Fi sound separately in postproduction, which is how professionals make their clips. Eight-mm video has this problem, too. The sound is recorded with the picture. Thus you can only record a music video in VHS or Beta Hi-Fi or in 8-mm if you make a performance video. You have to record the picture and the sound all at once, in one continuous shot.

If you have a Hi-Fi VCR, but don't want to make a performance video, you can use the regular audio track. Simply move the audio selection switch on the VCR to "normal audio" for playback and recording.

USING A CAMERA
OR CAMCORDER

All cameras and camcorders have many basic features in common. However, there are some optional features you might want to look for when you're choosing one to rent.

Auto-focus. If you're a beginner in shooting videos, this is definitely a feature you should consider. Like many photo cameras and binoculars, video cameras need to be *focused* according to the distance from the camera to your *subject.* With cameras without auto-focus, you have to turn the camera's focus ring until the picture looks sharp in your viewfinder. With auto-focus (which is short for "automatic focus"), this ring almost magically turns by itself. You don't have to worry about focusing; you just have to point the camera in the right direction.

Zoom. Zoom is a function that makes the camera look as if it has suddenly moved either close to the subject or far away. Used one way, a zoom lens gradually becomes more and more like a telescope, magnifying objects in the distance. This is called the *telephoto* effect. Used the other way, objects gradually look farther and farther away, in a *wide-angle* effect. Your camera will have either manual zoom controls, power zoom controls, or both. With manual zoom, you move a lever near the focus ring to make the camera zoom in or out. How fast it zooms depends on how quickly you move the lever. Cameras with power zoom have a tiny motor controlling the zoom function. Press the T (for "telephoto") button, and the camera will zoom in toward the subject. Press W (for "wide-angle") and the camera will zoom out, making the subject look farther away.

Fade-in and fade-out. A video picture fades in when a blank screen gradually turns into a picture. It fades out when the picture gradually disappears. Many video cameras have fade-in and fade-out. These techniques make a nice way of beginning and ending scenes.

Character generator. Here the word "character" means letter or number. "A" is a character and so is "6." Character generators are used to put titles and credits on a video movie. They are found only on very expensive, very complex cameras. You should look at the instruction manual for your video camera to see how your character generator works.

Titles can often help your video. "I Don't Want to Go Home, A Video by Kevin and Susie Hawkins" can make your audience more interested in the video that follows. If you don't have a character generator, you can still put a title on your program. Simply write the title in large letters on a piece of white cardboard and shoot it up close for a couple of seconds.

Other features you should know about are found on all video cameras. They include the following:

Iris. Video cameras and most home film cameras have automatic irises. They sense how much light is coming into the camera and adjust the iris opening. If there's a lot of light, the iris will close a little. If there's not, the iris will open wider.

Occasionally this iris adjustment won't be the adjustment that gives you the best picture. Say, for example, you are shooting someone standing in front of a window and sunlight is streaming in from that window. If you try to get a good picture of the person's face, the iris adjustment will be wrong; the person's face will be dark, completely in shadow.

Another use for the manual iris is as a substitute for fade-in and fade-out if your camera doesn't have that feature. If you gradually close the iris all the way when you're shooting, the picture will fade to black. If you open it gradually from a closed position when you begin the next scene, the picture will fade in again.

Remember to switch the iris back to automatic and to turn the backlight compensation off when you're back to normal shooting.

Color balance. Unlike our eyes and unlike film, video has some problems seeing colors correctly. If it's not corrected, a video camera may record a red shirt as red when it's indoors, but make the same shirt purple outdoors. Therefore, most video cameras have color controls that you must set.

The first control to set is the *color temperature control,* which is found on most cameras. "Temperature" here doesn't mean the same thing as the temperature in a weather forecast. Colors have a different kind of temperature. Red is a hot color, and blue is a very cool one. The light we get from the sun and from lamps is actually not white or clear. It's slightly colored. For instance, incandescent lights, the kind you find in most lamps, give off a yellowish light. Fluorescent lights—the long, skinny light bulbs you see in most schools—give a bluish light. Many cameras can't tell the difference between these kinds of light, so it's up to you to correct it.

The color temperature control will have either two or three positions. With this feature you will be able to choose between inside light and outside light, and sometimes between incandescent and fluorescent lights.

On most cameras, there's also a second control to set to make colors turn out right. This is the *white balance control.* You usually set it by holding a white piece of paper in front of the camera lens and then pushing the white balance button. When you push the button, you're telling the camera, "Look, *this* is white." The camera will then know how to recognize all the other colors, too. Be sure to set the color temperature control and the white balance (if your camera has one) *every time you set up a scene.*

Macro. "Macro" is a prefix that means "very large." The macro function on your video camera can make small objects look very large on the screen. If you decide your video should include a close-up of someone's eye, for example, turn the macro function on. This is usually done by turning one of the rings around the camera's lens. Remember to turn macro off when you finish shooting that scene.

Viewfinder. The viewfinder is the window you look through to see what kind of picture you're recording. Most video cameras today have black-and-white *electronic viewfinders.* These are actually miniature black-and-white TV screens. They show a small black-and-white version of what your picture will look like when you play it back on your TV set.

The other kind of viewfinder is a through-the-lens viewfinder, known as a *TTL viewfinder.* These viewfinders show you what the camera is pointing at by letting you look through the camera's lens. However, you don't see it exactly as it will appear on TV.

Viewfinder indications. When you look into your viewfinder, you'll see letters at the top or bottom of the picture. These are viewfinder indications. You should pay attention to them because they tell you whether the camera is working correctly. There should be one letter that lights up when the camera is recording. Another letter may light up if the white balance is wrong and needs to be adjusted. Another letter will tell you if your portable VCR's battery is running out of power and needs to be recharged. Before using the camera, look in the owner's manual to see what kind of viewfinder indications your camera has. Then watch for them when you begin to shoot.

Record/review. One advantage of having an electronic viewfinder on your camera is that you can use it to look at what you've already recorded, using it just like a tiny TV set. You usually do this by rewinding the VCR and setting the VCR/camera switches on the camera and VCR to "VCR." Then push the play button and you'll see your results in the viewfinder.

To make this whole process easier, many cameras have a feature called "record/review." After you finish taping a scene, you press the record/review button and the last few seconds of what you've shot will appear in the viewfinder. On some cameras, you don't have to press a button at all. When you stop taping, the last few seconds of footage automatically appear. This feature, as well as simply rewinding and then watching your footage, is useful for "editing in the camera," a technique we'll discuss a little later.

Microphone. While your camera is busy recording the video picture, the microphone on top of your camera records sound. Most cameras today have *unidirectional mikes.* ("Mike" is short for "microphone.") "Unidirectional" means "one direction." These mikes are designed to record sounds that come from the direction where the camera is pointed. So, if your actors are a bit far away from the microphone—say, 5 to 15 feet (1.5–4.6 m)—don't worry. The sounds will be picked up. If you're using the camera's microphone, however, the person operating the camera and the people nearby should make sure not to talk while taping is going on. You don't want to hear yourself saying "Oops, I moved the camera," in the middle of your video!

You can also record sound by using *external microphones.* These mikes are separate from your camera, connected to it by a cord. Using external mikes can give you better sound. Check to see if your camera has "external mike jacks" for plugging in extra microphones. Some cameras have one, for one mike, and some have two, for stereo recording with two microphones. You can record in stereo only if your portable VCR is stereo, too. If it's not, then just use one extra microphone. Extra microphones can be bought and sometimes rented at audio and music stores.

These microphones have long cords that allow you to put them close to your performers. Set up the mikes at table height about 3 to 6 feet (1–2 m) from the actors. If you're using two mikes, put them about 3 to 4 feet (91–121 cm) apart. If you don't have any microphone stands, Play-Dough makes a good substitute. Let your camera know that you'll be using the external mikes. If there is a microphone selector switch, turn it to "external" and, if you can, unplug the regular camera microphone and put it away in a safe place.

Most cameras have an earphone jack so that you can hear what you're recording through earphones. Instead of using the little earphone that comes with your camera, try using the earphones from a Walkman or portable stereo. These stay on your head more easily and sound better, too.

There are a few more things you should know and remember about video cameras and camcorders.

1. *Never* point a video camera directly at the sun or at a bright light. Almost all cameras today use something called a *pickup tube* to register the picture information. If this tube is exposed to too much bright light, it can get "burned in." From then on, a ghostly image of that bright light will show up in every picture you shoot.

2. Put the lens cap back on the camera when you are finished with it. This prevents the lens from getting scratched and those scratches from showing up in your picture!

3. A video camera is a *very* expensive, delicate piece of equipment. Whether it belongs to your family, the local video store, or your school, treat it carefully and with respect.

Making a video movie requires power. This power is provided by the *rechargeable battery* in the VCR or camcorder.

Rechargeable batteries are different from the kind of battery you use with a flashlight or a Walkman. When rechargeable batteries run out of energy, they can be charged up again with help from the electricity that comes from a wall socket. You recharge a portable VCR battery by reconnecting the portable part of the VCR to the tuner/timer, which is plugged into the wall. You recharge a camcorder battery with the help of an adapter that should come with it. A light tells you when the battery is all charged up.

VIDEO TAPE

Because there are so many different brands and types of video tape for sale, it can be confusing to shop for tape. As long as you get tape that's the right format for your equipment—VHS, VHS-C, Beta, or 8-mm—you won't go wrong.

Besides labels for format, video tape usually has a label for quality. Ordinary-quality video tape is usually called *standard grade* while the more expensive, better-quality types are often called *high grade, extra high grade*, or *super high grade*. A more expensive grade of video tape will give you a slightly better picture, but don't worry if you can't afford it. The standard grade is good, too.

VHS and Beta tape comes in different lengths. In VHS, a *T-120* cassette will give you two hours of recording time at the SP speed. In Beta, an *L-500* will give you two hours at the Beta II speed. Two hours is more than long enough for shooting a music video. If you're using a VHS-C camcorder, you should buy *TC-20* tapes, which will give you twenty to sixty minutes of playing time, depending on what type of camcorder you have.

There are two kinds of 8-mm video tape: *MP* (which stands for "metal particle") and *ME* ("metal evaporated"). It's best to buy the type recommended in the owner's manual for the camcorder you're using.

More important than what kind of video tape you buy is how you take care of it. Moisture, heat, and dust are the enemies of video tape. Keep your cassettes dry and don't leave them in the sun or in a locked car where they will get too hot. Most important, don't get them dirty. Even tiny amounts of dust on the tape can mess up the picture with ugly streaks and specks. Never open the cassette or touch the tape inside. And keep the cassette in the box it came in when you're not using it.

TRIPODS

You may want to use a *tripod* for your video if one is available to you. A tripod is a three-legged stand for a camera or camcorder. A tripod will be helpful if you're going to be shooting in one place for a long time, for example, if you're taping a friend sitting in a chair and playing a song on the guitar. Video cameras and camcorders *are* heavy; they can weigh from two to eight pounds (.9 to 3.6 kg). A tripod gives you a better chance of getting a steady shot.

USING FILM EQUIPMENT

Home film equipment is a miniature version of the equipment used to make the movies you see in the theater. The makers of those movies use film that's 35 mm wide (almost 1.4 inches) and sometimes 70 mm wide (2.8 inches). Home movie cameras handle film that's 8-mm (.3 inch) wide.

There are two kinds of home movie cameras. Their names sound alike, but they work slightly differently. They are Super 8 and 8-mm.

Super 8 film and *8-mm film* are the same width. However, Super 8 squeezes a slightly wider picture onto the film, which is why it's called "super." If you have a Super 8 camera, you must buy Super 8 film. If you have an 8-mm camera, you must buy 8-mm film. This difference isn't so important when it comes time to play your finished film. Most projectors will play both types of film.

FILM CAMERAS

Like a still photo camera, a movie camera has a lens that concentrates the light entering the camera on the film. In order to make the image sharp, the person operating the camera has to *focus* the lens on the object being shot. This is done by looking through the camera's viewfinder, the small window that lets you see what the lens is seeing, and turning a ring near the front of the lens until the picture becomes sharp.

Most film cameras also have an automatic iris. Just as the iris in your eye gets smaller to keep too much light from entering your eye on bright days, the camera's iris regulates how much light reaches the film. To help the iris do this job, most cameras also have a *brightness switch* that tells it whether you are shooting indoors, outdoors on a cloudy day, or outdoors on a sunny day.

A third control is zoom. Like the zoom control on a video camera, a film camera zoom controls how much the lens magnifies the image. Therefore, it can make it appear as if the camera is moving toward or away from the subject. Many cameras have both manual and power zoom controls. Manual zoom is operated with a lever near the camera's focus ring. Moving it in one direction makes everything in the picture seem close; moving it in the other makes objects appear small and distant. Power zoom is operated by pushing one of two buttons. The T (telephoto) button zooms the camera up close; the W (wide-angle) button zooms it away.

A few types of Super 8 movie cameras can record sound while they shoot the picture. One type records sound on a narrow strip at the edge of the film. (Be sure to buy Super 8 *sound* film if you are using this type of camera.) The other type uses a special audio tape recorder, connected to the camera, that turns on and off whenever the camera does.

If your film camera can't record sound, don't worry. It's not necessary for your music video. If you or a friend have a portable audio cassette player, it will work fine for playing back the sound for your clip, as long as you start playing the song and the clip at the same time. If you are making a conceptual video, you'll need a portable tape recorder whether you're using video, film with sound, or film without sound. The tape player provides the background music during the shoot, so that the actors know what part of the song they're acting out. We discuss this further in chapter six.

FILM

Super 8 film comes in color and black and white. Though color film is much more popular for home movies, you might want to experiment with black and white for your video, especially when you are just learning to use the camera. For one thing, black-and-white film is usually less expensive to buy and develop. Shooting in black and white can also give your video the same mysterious look professional video directors get when they use black and white.

You buy and use super 8 film in the form of cartridges that hold either 50 feet (15 m) of film—two and a half to three minutes of shooting—or 200 feet (61 m)—about eleven minutes. Color film costs up to fifteen dollars per cartridge for 50 feet and forty dollars for 200 feet. Black and white costs up to ten dollars per 50-foot cartridge. The cartridges pop right into the camera; to load it, you never need to touch the film. The 8-mm film comes in rolls, which are a bit trickier to load.

Movie film comes in different *ASA* ratings, ranging from 40 to 200. (These are also called ISO ratings.) The ASA rating tells how sensitive the film is to light, and thus, how much light you'll need to make a picture with it. For color, ASA 40 film is a good all-around film for both outdoor and indoor shooting. For black and white, ASA 100 is good for shooting in bright sunlight. The less light you have, the closer your ASA should be to 200. Whatever ASA rating you use, be sure to set the small ASA adjustment on the camera to the same number as the ASA rating of the film you're using.

4
USING YOUR EQUIPMENT

Before you start shooting—or even writing—your video, it's important that you practice using your equipment. A good way to do this is to make a sample tape or film, trying out various shooting techniques and camera controls. Not only will you learn how the equipment works, you'll learn what it can do. This will make it easier for you to write a video script that will look as good on the screen as it does on paper.

If you're using a film camera, practice loading the cartridge and turning the camera on and off. Then practice shooting, framing your subject in the viewfinder and following someone in action. Use the focus, zoom, and brightness controls to see what kind of effects they give you. Make sure you develop the practice film before you write your video. Watch the film for mistakes to avoid and good effects to include in the script.

Video equipment is a bit more complex. Thus, before you shoot, you should practice setting up the equipment. If you have the camera's owner's manual, use it to help you locate all the camera controls.

If you're using a camera and a portable VCR, the first thing to do is make sure you have a cable that connects them. It will be at least 5 feet (1.5 m) in length and have a *multipin connector* (a plug with many little pins) on each end. One of these connectors plugs into the camera, the other into the VCR. Unless the person at the video store gives you different instructions, it doesn't matter which end you plug into which piece of equipment. Beta VCRs use plugs with fourteen pins. So, if you're using a Beta VCR, you should have a camera that takes a fourteen-pin connector, too. VHS VCRs use ten-pin connectors, so the camera you connect to a VHS VCR should also use a ten-pin plug.

The cord between the camera and the VCR sends the picture (video) and the sound (audio) to the VCR to be recorded. It also sends instructions from the camera to the VCR, for example, instructions to start and stop recording. A fourth, very important function of this cord is to send power from the battery in the VCR to the camera.

When you've got your camera and VCR or camcorder, and a fully charged battery, all set up, then it's time to start practicing. Pop a blank video cassette in the VCR and make sure that it's rewound. Then set your color temperature controls and white balance so that the colors in your recording come out right. Now you're ready to start shooting.

Find the "run" button on your camera. It should be within easy reach of one of your fingers when you're holding the camera by the hand grip. This button tells the camera to start and stop recording. Now, looking through the viewfinder, aim the camera at a subject, perhaps a friend. Leave plenty of room at the edges of the frame for your friend to move about. Then, when you're sure you're ready, press the run button.

As you're shooting, have your friend walk slowly across the room. Try to follow this movement with your camera. If you have an auto-focus camera, the camera will do the focusing itself. If you don't have auto-focus, practice focusing, getting as sharp a picture as you can in the viewfinder as your subject moves toward and away from you.

Next, try the zoom control. See what kind of effect this gives to the picture and think about whether you'd want to use an effect like this in your music video.

Try out all the controls on the camera for this sample tape. Keep trying until you think you've mastered the techniques. When you've finished a long practice session, play back the tape on TV. Note the mistakes you've made (things that look awkward or funny, like cutting off the tops of people's heads in the frame). Also note the things that look good—an interesting angle on someone's face, for example, or a close-up of an everyday object like an orange. Keep what you've learned in mind when planning your video.

One other technique you'll want to think about when you write your script is *editing in the camera.* Editing is the process of weeding out the shots you don't want and keeping only the parts you do want. Normally, editing is done after the shoot is all finished. As we said earlier, it's much more difficult to do this with video than it is with film. Editing in the camera is a way to avoid having to edit later with video at all.

In normal, after-the-shoot film editing, film editors actually hold the developed film in their hands and look at it to decide which frames should stay and which should be taken out. The unwanted footage is cut out and the wanted film is simply taped together. If you're using film for your video, you'll edit this way. After-the-shoot video editing is more difficult because you can't hold video tape in your hands and tell what pictures you're looking at. A video editor can only tell what's on a tape by playing it back on a VCR and a TV. And editing is done by feeding the pictures you want from the original tape to a blank tape on a second VCR. With home video equipment, the cut between one transferred scene and another is often not smooth. A horizontal black line, called a *roll,* frequently appears in the middle of the screen and travels up to the top.

Editing in the camera helps you avoid this whole process. With this technique, you record *only the scenes you want in the first place.* It works because with video tape, as with audio tape, you can rewind a tape that has one scene on it, tape a second scene on the same

By turning off and on your camera, you can create special effects. Here the performer is lying on the couch. By turning off the camera and then turning it on again after he leaves the couch, it looks like he suddenly disappeared.

part of the tape the first scene is on, and the first scene will disappear completely.

This technique is perfect for shooting a music video according to a script. After you shoot a scene, rewind the tape and watch what you've just shot in the electronic viewfinder. (If you don't have an electronic viewfinder, you can hook up your VCR to a TV while you're shooting.) If you like what you've just shot, then stop the tape at the end of that scene and go on to shooting the next one. But if you *don't* like what you've shot, you can edit that scene out. Simply rewind the tape to the end of the previous scene. Then begin shooting again.

You can also use editing in the camera to fool your audience with illusions and special effects. For example, say you wanted to show a scene in which your little sister accidentally drops an expensive ring in a pond. You would shoot a few seconds of her playing with the ring near the water. You would follow that with a close-up shot of the water surface broken by the splash of a small stone or other object. You could make this scene look most realistic by editing in the camera. After you shoot the scene of your sister playing, rewind it and watch closely in the viewfinder or monitor to see when she looks most like she's about to drop the ring. Then rewind the tape and stop it at that point, and shoot the splash in the water. You will have "edited out" the last part of the first scene. Only the first part—the part you want—will be left.

Editing in the camera can also be used for magic tricks and other special effects. You can make a friend "disappear" by first shooting him or her in one place—sitting on a couch, for example—then stopping the camera and having your friend get up and out of the camera's sight. Then shoot the couch with no one on it. When you play this tape back, it will look as if your friend just disappeared.

5 PLANNING YOUR VIDEO

Once you've learned to operate your equipment, then the real excitement begins. Planning your music video clip takes thought and organization, but it can also be fun.

WHO'S IN CHARGE?

Because it takes many people to make a video, you'll need a lot of friends to work on the video together. Some may be involved from the beginning. Others may join you only when the shooting begins. However many people are working together from the beginning, though, you'll need to put people in charge, as the professionals do. Specifically, you'll need a producer, a director, a cameraperson, and a sound person. The people who take on these jobs won't be in the video, but without them you won't be able to make it at all.

    As in professional videos, the producer's job is to take care of all business, scheduling, and other details of your video production. The producer arranges when and where the shooting will take place and asks permission if necessary. He or she chooses the day for the shoot and makes sure that everyone will be there. The producer is also in charge of the money for the production: for renting equipment, buying video and audio tape, buying or renting props and costumes, and any other expenses that come up. (You might want to work out a system in which everyone working on the video contributes dues to cover the expenses.) Of course, the producer doesn't have to do all this alone. But even with assistants, the producer should still be in charge and responsible for all these things.

The director is responsible for the creative aspects of the video. He or she decides what will look best in the camera and makes sure the video is done that way. The director decides where on the set all the actors should stand. Should Julie be standing right in front of Alan when they're supposed to be arguing or should they stand a few feet away from each other? Should an extra walk toward John as he strolls down the sidewalk or should someone walk past him, in the same direction, to show how slowly he's going? With the help of others, the director designs the set and oversees its building, judging all the time what would look best in the camera. Deciding how costumes should look is also one of the director's responsibilities, although a friend with a sense of fashion could certainly help out.

The cameraperson is responsible for the operation and care of the camera and all related equipment. He or she should be technically minded and also strong enough to hold the camera for long periods of time with a steady hand. If you're renting equipment, he or she should go to the video or photography store with the producer to pick it out. They both should listen carefully to the suggestions and advice of the people there. The cameraperson follows the director's instructions when shooting, but should feel free to make alternative suggestions if a scene the director sets up doesn't look good in the camera's viewfinder.

Depending on how you decide to shoot your video—as a performance or conceptual clip—the sound person's job will vary. Basically, however, he or she is responsible for all aspects of the video's sound, from start to finish. If you're doing a performance video, the sound person will set up the microphones. If you're doing a conceptual shoot, the sound person is responsible for playing back your song on a portable audio tape recorder during the shooting, making sure the right part of the song is playing for each different shot and scene. The sound person should consult the script throughout the shoot. When the shooting is all done, he or she is responsible for transferring the original audio onto the audio track of the video tape.

WHAT ABOUT THE MUSIC?

The first step in planning the video itself is to decide what kind of music you're going to use. Are you or any of your friends musicians? Do you like to sing? If so, you can make a video you can be seen and heard in. Perhaps one of you has written a song. You can use that. Otherwise, pick one of your favorite songs to play and sing.

If you don't want to play music yourselves, you can pick one of your favorite rock or pop or other songs from a record or tape. The music you choose will determine how you should set up the shoot. If you use a professional song, you can't play your video in public or get paid anything for playing it unless you get permission from the record company first, even if you've recorded the song off the radio.

There are two ways of making a video with music you perform yourselves. You can record the music either while you're shooting the action or before you shoot. The first way would give you a performance video; the second, a conceptual video. Unless you have a film camera system that records picture *and* sound, you'll have to use video to make a performance video. You can make a conceptual video with either film or video.

Because you can't interrupt the recording of a song without making the song sound funny, a performance video has to be recorded in all one shot, or take—no turning the camera on and off in the middle.

Thus, during a performance shoot, you have to get everything perfect at once. If everyone acting in the video is getting the "moves" down perfectly on one particular take, and then someone forgets the words, you have to shoot the whole thing over again. On the other hand, recording picture and sound together is your best guarantee that the actions and the music will be "in synch." You won't have people's mouths saying one thing while a different part of the song is coming out of the speakers.

Getting "out of synch" is the biggest danger when you record the music before you record the video. Professionals use very sophisticated "synching" equipment to make sure actions and music happen at the right time. This is not really possible with home video or film equipment. Thus we don't recommend having the actors lip-synch the words to the song in a homemade conceptual video. Recording the music before the shoot, however, will allow you to include many different scenes in your video, just like in professional conceptual videos.

To use your own music, first record the song on an audio tape recorder. Be sure to use an external microphone, not a mike that's built into the recorder. An external mike will give you the best sound. As with a professionally recorded song, the sound person plays back the song while the scene is being shot to get actors moving to the beat and to time certain actions to certain phrases in the song. When you're finished shooting, you'll transfer the song onto the video tape in order to get a tape that plays sound and picture together.

PROJECTING AN IMAGE

Whether you choose to make a performance or a conceptual video, play the music yourselves or use professional music, you'll need to think of a way to present your video to the audience.

For a performance video, you'll need a setting, costumes, and a basic idea about what kind of image the band wants to project. Look at the different performers you see on TV. Heavy-metal bands like

Kiss seem to be aggresssive and menacing. Duran Duran, on the other hand, is slick, sophisticated, and cute. Other bands in the past, for example, the Australian band Men at Work, have tried to project an image of goofiness. These images do not represent what the band members are really like. Rather, bands put on an act on stage in order to entertain the audience better and to help the audience remember them as something special—people different from the average person.

Ask your musicians what kind of image they'd like to project. The image should go along with the song. Then carry that theme through in clothes, scenery, and actions. Real rockers could dress up in "loud" clothes à la Spinal Tap. Those who sing sweet, mellow songs should dress in mellow clothes and act mellow, too. Country musicians could wear cowboy hats, jeans, and bandanas.

USING SCENERY

Good in-concert scenery is sometimes difficult for a home video maker to find, but you'll get best results if you're creative. If there's not enough space for a good-sized stage in your or a friend's home, perhaps you could borrow the stage at your school or your local Y. Then try to turn that space into an attractive set. Music video director Martin Kahan, who made Ricky Skaggs's "I'm Just a Country Boy" video, suggests that one of the best—and least expensive—ways to set up a video is to use established sets—sets that were already used by someone else. He tells of saving thousands of dollars on a set for a video for Bruce Springsteen's saxophonist Clarence Clemons. Kahan found a set of the White House in a studio in New York. He got the idea of making Clemons president of the United States in his video. If your school puts on plays, you'll probably find some scenery that you can borrow. Sometimes parts of old sets sit forgotten in school storerooms. Ask permission to poke around in them. You may be surprised at what you find.

*Young star Julian Lennon prefers
simple videos that highlight his
songwriting and singing.*

If you can't find scenery, you can make your own. Just putting someone in front of a curtain can look better than putting them in front of a bare wall. Different members of the band could also stand on risers (platforms) of different heights. And lighting can create vastly different moods on the same set. (See chapter six for more information on lighting.) Scenery can also be people. You should decide whether to have an audience watching and cheering on the performance.

PLANNING THE MOVES

The moves of every performer during a performance video should be planned out, or *choreographed,* as dancers say. You can't just have band members spontaneously running around the set doing whatever they want, because the cameraperson has to know what they're going to do in order to follow their movements. A video is really like a dance between the performers and the camera. If the lead singer has a particularly strong line in the song, like "You ain't seen nothing yet," you should plan to have that performer look into the camera lens while singing it. (It will look like he or she is looking right into the audience's eyes.) Your cameraperson should be ready to go in for a close-up at that point. All performer and camera movements should be included in the script, which we discuss in the next section.

Conceptual videos take even more planning than performance videos do. A conceptual video is like a miniature play or movie without words. When you're writing it, you'll need to make up characters and put them in a situation. Raven's "On and On" video, discussed in chapter two, was about three musicians (Raven) who had a hard time getting a recording contract. When they finally became famous, they got back at the record company executive. Michael Jackson's classic "Beat It" video was about a gang fight that was broken up by the power of music.

As you can see from the examples just mentioned, the concept doesn't necessarily have to be related to the words in the song. If you've got a song with a strong theme, you should try to use it. For example, a song about a train should probably have scenes of a train or at least a train station in the video. But if your song has no theme that is easily illustrated, you can write a video about any situation you feel like depicting. In either case, it's not necessary that the video act out the song word for word. This can get corny.

As you work on ideas for your conceptual video, you should examine your resources, as we suggested you do with the performance video. Did someone in your school just put on a play with some elaborate scenery you could borrow? Do you or someone you know have some great costumes you could use? (One hoop skirt could lead to doing a music video version of *Gone with the Wind*.) Take these things into consideration, as you start thinking up concepts.

It's most fun to have lots of people coming up with ideas for your video. One way of doing this that is used by a lot of businesses is called "brainstorming." During brainstorming, everyone sits around in a circle. One person has pen and paper. Then, everyone begins throwing out ideas—all sorts of ideas, no matter how silly or even impossible to do they might seem. Hearing other people's ideas often helps you think up your own. The person with the paper writes down *all* the ideas. Only when everyone is all out of ideas do you start evaluating them. Decide whether or not most of you like each idea and whether it would be possible to do a video for it. To decide whether it's possible, ask yourselves these questions:

• How many people would you need for the clip? How many people do you have? (Remember, you'll probably need at least four technical people who won't be in the clip at all.)

• What kind of scenery would you need? If the clip would be shot outside, but it's now snowy or cold, it might be best to wait until spring. If it's inside, is there a room in one of your houses that would make a good background? Would your parents let you shoot there?

• What costumes would you need for the shoot? Get into the Halloween spirit: See if you can make or borrow the right kind of costumes. If you've got enough people and the right kind of scenery and costumes, then you're ready to move on. It's time to write the *script*.

WRITING THE SCRIPT

Take a look at the excerpt from the script for "On and On" in chapter two. It's very detailed; it tells *everything* that happens in that portion of the video clip. When it came time to make the video, there wasn't a big hole in the middle of the song where a picture should be.

Though it may not be as long or as complex, your script should be as complete as this one is. What you should aim for is to make sure there are pictures to go with every part of your song.

Though it's a good idea to have a lot of people thinking up the concept, it's difficult to have a lot of people writing a script. Have only one or two people write the original script—perhaps your friends who like to write the most. Everyone else involved can read it over and come up with suggestions for improvements. These suggestions should be discussed to decide whether they should be incorporated. Then the original writer or writers could go back and write up a final version.

Like the script in chapter two, yours should be written in two columns. At the top of the page, make two headings: "Song" and "Actions." In the song column, map out the song. If there's an introduction, write "Introduction." Then write out the words to the song. If there's a musical interlude, or "break," during the song, be sure to indicate that. Also note if there's a musical ending to the song.

When you've got the song all mapped out, then you can start planning the actions. Say you're using a song about throwing a dance party. During the introduction, you could set up the scene. Across from "Introduction," you could write: "House set back from street without anyone in front of it." Then think of some action for when the words start. As the singers chant, "If you feel like taking a chance, c'mon over to my house and dance," you can have a mail carrier walking by the house suddenly drop the mail bag and run toward the house. Set up the script like this:

SONG: "Dance, Dance, Dance"	ACTIONS
Introduction: Nah, nah, nah, nah, nah, nah, nah, nah, nah, nah, nah, nah, nah, nah, nah, nah, nah, nah, nah, nah, nah, nah, nah, NAH——	House set back from street without anyone in front of it. Camera zooms in toward window which reveals people dancing behind it.
If you feel like taking a chance	Mail carrier in front of house. He quickly turns his head to look at house, then looks back in front of him, surprised.
c'mon over to my house and dance.	He drops his bag and starts running toward the house.

One very important part of a script is the description of *camera angles*. The script should tell whether the camera is looking at the person from close up or far away, from the subject's left or right, and even whether it's looking at the person from below or from the top of a ladder. Next time you watch a video clip, a movie, or a TV show, notice how many different camera angles you see in a few minutes' time. Each different angle gives a different point of view on the subjects in the video. Changing camera angles makes a video more interesting to watch. It also makes it more informative. If one of the characters is supposed to be looking upset, this can be conveyed much more effectively by a close-up of the face than by a wide shot from far away.

There are basically four kinds of *shots* in video: *wide shots, medium shots, close-up shots,* and *extreme close-up shots.* Wide

shots take in the whole scene—the area they cover is wide. Medium shots come in a little closer on the subject. Medium shots show people from about their waists up. Close-ups show just one person—from the bottom of the neck up. And extreme close-ups show just the face or less—sometimes just eyes, nose, and mouth, and not the forehead or hair.

These shots each have a different function in telling a story. Wide shots are important as *establishing shots*—shots that establish for the viewers where the video is taking place. An establishing wide shot should be used at the beginning or *very* close to the beginning of every scene. Wide shots can, of course, also be used throughout the video, especially in scenes where a lot of people are running around doing different things.

The medium shot, being the middle-range shot, is used most often in TV. Use it to cover smaller patches of action and for one person talking or singing to another. The close-up is more dramatic; it's not used for general action, it's used to illustrate something. It could be someone's face expressing a strong emotion, or an object that's significant to the action, for example, a key or a lost glass slipper. An extreme close-up is even more dramatic. It's used for many of the same things the close-up is, but it shouldn't be used too often.

Above left: wide shots, like this one, cover a wide area. They take in the whole scene. Above right: medium shots focus on one or two people from the knees or waist up. Below left: a close-up shot focuses just on a person's head, usually from the shoulders or neck up. Below right: An extreme close-up shot covers just the face, often only the eyes, nose, and mouth, without showing the whole head.

In choreographing shots for your video, don't move from a really wide shot to a really close shot and vice versa. It's too disorienting to the viewer. Instead, get the viewer from a wide shot to a close shot in steps: put a medium shot in the middle. Also, don't keep the camera at the same angle when you're changing shots. Otherwise the camera will look like it is jumping toward or away from the subject.

Of course, if you're doing a performance video in a continuous shoot (one take), you won't be able to switch from shot to shot, switching in between. You can vary camera angles by having the cameraperson walk slowly and carefully about the set while shooting and by using the zoom and moving the camera on the tripod. However, you should not use the zoom too often—it will look silly and amateurish.

There are other camera techniques that can help tell a story. A *pan* is a shot that moves horizontally, from one part of a set to another. If the cameraperson has been holding a medium shot on the bass player in your group and it's time to transfer attention to the lead guitarist, a pan is what gets you from here to there.

A *defocus shot* is another way of making transitions. You move the camera lens from being in focus to being blurry. If you're using an auto-focus camera, you'll need to switch the auto/manual focus switch to manual before turning the focus ring yourself. A defocus shot can be used between scenes in a conceptual video or, if the cameraperson is skillful, between shots in a continuously shot performance video.

One of the most exciting types of shots is called a *dolly shot*. Professional video producers often put the camera and the cameraperson on a wheeled platform called a dolly. This lets them move the camera around while shooting. You can do the same thing by putting your cameraperson in a wheeled cart, a wagon, an office chair with wheels, or even a wheelchair.

Assign one person on your crew to move the dolly (and the cameraperson in it, of course) toward or away from the action in the shot. For example, if your actors are walking toward the camera, pull the dolly *backward* so that the distance between the camera and the actors stays the same. If you're doing this on a sidewalk or bumpy ground, lay down some boards for the dolly to roll on more smoothly.

Be sure to illustrate all important elements of the story in your conceptual video. If someone proposes marriage or even hits or punches someone, be sure to include a shot of that person's reaction—happy or hurt.

These *reaction shots* appear all the time in TV shows, movies, and rock videos. They help make the viewers feel more involved with what's happening on the screen.

It's also important to show clearly all the little details that help tell the story. If someone hands a person a key—say to a haunted house—be sure to get a close-up of the key for a few seconds.

Every action in the scene should include the camera angle. The cameraperson should have a copy of the script to study for each scene. However, because it would be difficult to memorize all the shots, you might want to appoint an assistant to remind the cameraperson of what is coming next.

Thus, the final script to the video above should start something like this:

SONG: "Dance, Dance, Dance"	ACTIONS
Introduction: Nah, nah, nah, nah, nah, nah, nah, nah, nah, nah, nah, nah, nah, nah, nah, nah, nah, nah, nah, nah, nah, nah, nah, NAH——	Wide shot of house set back from street without anyone in front of it. Camera zooms in toward window, revealing people in crazy, punky costumes dancing behind it.
If you feel like taking a chance,	Medium shot of mail carrier in front of house, on sidewalk. (House is in back of him, to the right.) He quickly turns his head to look at house, then

looks back in front of him, toward camera, surprised.

c'mon over to my house and dance.

Medium shot: Mail carrier drops his bag and starts running toward the house.

If you feel like having some fun,

Medium shot, from across counter, straight in front of her, of chef in white clothes and floppy white hat. She is kneading a big ball of dough.

c'mon over, don't walk, run. RUN!

Medium shot: She stops kneading, looks surprised. Then, she throws the dough up in the air and runs out of the picture. The scene stops *before* the dough comes back down.

Put on your best clothes and your best shoes.

Medium shot from his left of a fisherman in hip waders sitting on the bank of a river, lake, or pond. He's holding a shaking fishing pole that looks like it has a fighting fish on the end. He looks excited.

We're having a party, start spreading the news.

Medium shot: He suddenly turns toward camera with his mouth open, looking *really* excited. He throws fishing pole into the water.

If you feel like taking a chance, c'mon over to my house and dance.

Mail carrier, chef (still in white and covered with flour), and fisherman (still in waders) are

	running along sidewalk toward house. Cameraperson is crouched down near sidewalk with camera pointed up toward their faces. They run toward the camera, then past it.
And dance (wear your best clothes and your best pants)	Wide shot. Inside the playroom. Many people dancing, including the people with the punky clothes and the mail carrier, chef, and fisherman. (Flour flies when the chef dances.)
And dance (get out of your chair and take a chance) And dance dance dance dance DANCE!	Medium shot of mail carrier doing a break-dancing move. Close-up of person in sequined hat, dancing. Close-up of mail carrier dancing. Close-up of chef dancing. Close-up of fisherman dancing. Wide shot of everyone at the party dancing their hearts out.

If you're having a hard time getting started on your script—or even if you're not—a *storyboard* is a good way to begin getting some ideas. Often used by directors making TV ads, a storyboard is like a comic strip of the program you're going to create. As the example on page 62 shows, you don't have to be a good artist to make a storyboard. Sometimes just drawing a storyboard can give you ideas on how the video should look and what the actors should do. Your storyboard could be very detailed or not detailed at all. That is, it could depict every action that will take place on screen or just depict generally what each set will look like. Instead of using squares, as comic strip

artists do, you should draw your storyboard in miniature TV screens. The boxes should reflect the proportions of a TV screen—wider than it is tall and rounded at the corners. (The "screen" should be four units wide by three units high.) Cut out a piece of cardboard for a stencil and use it to draw all your boxes on paper.

PREPARING FOR THE SHOOT

Once you've finished writing your video, it's time to start bringing the script to life. Step one is picking the cast. Go through your whole script and write down all the characters you need. Don't leave anyone out. Don't forget the extras. If your star is going to be walking down a sidewalk by herself looking glum, then you'll need some people to walk past her, going in both directions. If you're going to be shooting a class at school, you'll need lots of students. You should choose your stars on the basis of whether they can do the acting required and whether they "look the part." If your video will require some good acting, for example, someone who can cry very realistically, you might want to have auditions to see who cries the best.

Every cast, of course, needs costumes. Think about the details in the costumes that might make a difference on screen. For example, if you're shooting a video about the last day of school, make sure your actors are wearing summer clothes—even if you're shooting indoors in the middle of winter!

A storyboard is a kind of cartoon showing all the scenes in a video. Drawing a storyboard like this one will help you plan how to shoot your video.

One thing to remember about choosing costumes is that color matters with video. Some colors just aren't good to wear on TV. Video does not like a lot of contrasts. It does not do a good job on black-and-white outfits, for example. It also can't pick up bright colors like red, orange, yellow, and lime green without looking funny. If you ever see a person wearing bright red on TV, look closely. The color will move, like rippling water. Your actors should also wear costumes that don't contrast too much with their skin. For example, white people should not wear very dark clothes, and black people should not wear very light clothes.

This same principle applies to scenery. Try not to use backgrounds that are too bright or have "busy" patterns, like boldly striped wallpaper. Otherwise your camera will have to work too hard to handle the contrast between the actors and the background and you won't get as good a picture.

Set up your scenery carefully. The *set* should not be too crowded. If you're taping inside, don't have too many pieces of furniture on the set or too many props around (unless you want a really cluttered look). Keep your script in mind. Rehearse the video in your head as you're setting up the set for little details that might make the difference. In the Raven video discussed in chapter two, the set was supposed to be the office of a record company. The set designers had remembered a sign with the name of the company and posters of rock and roll bands on the walls. But the company's executive's desk, around which most of the action was taking place, was bare except for a few papers. Someone suddenly said, "Hey, this is supposed to be a record company. Shouldn't there be records or something on the desk?" There were no record stores in the area and no records in the studio. Finally, a production assistant remembered she'd brought some cassette tapes for her Walkman, so the office looked like a record company office after all!

6

THE SHOOT

The big day has finally arrived. You've got your script, your technical staff, your equipment, your cast, your costumes, your sets. After days, even weeks, of planning, you're ready to shoot. Now it's time.

Music videos make an enjoyable three minutes of watching, but they usually require several hours of shooting. The music videos you see on TV take anywhere from one long day to a week to shoot. The more sets you have in one video and the more shots you've written into your script, the longer it takes. Each scene has to be set up anew.

But even if you're doing only one scene and one shot, it can still take a long time. When we shot a performance video with some musician friends, it took an entire afternoon to get a take that pleased all of us. So . . . come to the set with a lot of patience for the slow process and for your co-workers. After all, if too many arguments erupt, you won't get anything done!

WHAT SCENES TO SHOOT FIRST

How your shoot proceeds will depend on what kind of video you've planned. If you're doing a performance video, recording picture and sound all at once, you'll do one continuous shoot of the whole song so that the sound is free of interruptions. The nice thing about shooting on video is that you can do take after take on the same tape, without rewinding. When you've done enough takes that you're pleased with, you can play them all back to see which you like best. If you're shooting on film, on the other hand, it can get very expensive to shoot many takes, so make sure the performers are well rehearsed before turning on the camera.

Conceptual videos involve a lot more organization to shoot. They usually involve shooting many different scenes—in one or many sets—one after another. Professional music-video makers shoot the scenes in their conceptual videos in the order that's most convenient for them. If scene one takes place in the living room, scene two in the dining room, and scene three back in the living room, they'll shoot scenes one and three first and scene two later to avoid having to move too much equipment around. If you're shooting on film, you should organize your shooting schedule this way. After the film is developed, you'll be able to rearrange the footage in the right order. For video, however, we recommend that you shoot the scenes in the order they appear in the script, so that you can use the editing-in-the-camera technique described on page 43. When you finally finish shooting the whole script, you'll have a complete video (except for sound) on your tape. Editing after a shoot with video, as we've

Many music videos are supposed to look like scenes from the movies. Madonna's "Material Girl" video, for example is based on a scene from a Marilyn Monroe movie called Gentlemen Prefer Blondes.

said, is quite complicated and requires two VCRs. Often, the results aren't as good as editing with film. Editing in the camera will allow you to redo scenes as you shoot them, but you won't be able to go back and change a scene after you've finished the whole tape.

WHAT ABOUT LIGHTING?

The shoot begins with setting up the scene. And whether you're indoors or outdoors, it begins with thinking about the lighting.

Just as your eyes need light to see, a camera needs light to record. But you should not let your eyes be the judge of how much light there should be, because your camera needs a lot more.

All video cameras are different, and some need a lot more light than others. If you have your owner's manual handy, you can get an idea of how much light your camera needs by looking up its *minimum illumination*. Minimum illumination is the least light a camera needs to make a good picture. It is measured in *lux*. Cameras with minimum illumination of less than 30 lux need only normal room light to operate. Cameras that need more than 60 lux should only be used in very bright light. With most cameras, you can tell if there's too little light because an "L" will flash in the viewfinder. Without enough light, the camera will probably still see the picture, but when you play back your video, it will look dim and almost colorless.

If you're shooting with a film camera, it's even more important to have enough light. Without it, pictures come out looking dark and murky. Most film cameras also have a warning light in the viewfinder to tell when there's not enough light.

When you're setting up light for your shoot, you want to make sure (1) that there's enough light and (2) that the light makes your subjects look good.

If you're shooting outside on a relatively sunny day, you probably have enough light without adding any extra. It's inside that you have to worry about having enough. The place to start adding light to a scene is with the light fixtures already in the room. Most will probably have 60- and 75-watt bulbs. By replacing these with 150- and even

250-watt bulbs, you can bring much more light into the room. (You can get these bulbs at most hardware stores.) Another way of bringing light into a room is to buy inexpensive "scoop" lights at the hardware store. These usually have a clamp by which they can be attached to shelves, tables, and other surfaces, and then pointed at the subject. Remember, with the stronger bulbs and the new lights, you're going to be drawing more power. You don't want to overload the circuits in the room and blow a fuse or trip a circuit breaker. Don't try to plug too many lights into each socket or into one extension cord. Instead, spread the lights around to different sockets in the room, and if you run out, use a long extension cord to bring in power from another room.

Windows, expecially on a nice sunny day, bring in a lot of light. But sometimes they bring in too much. As we discussed on page 32, when a camera is pointed at a subject *and* a bright background, it will adjust itself for the background and leave the subject in shadows. Light coming in from outside can also make some of the colors in your video look strange. Remember what we said about different kinds of light having different color temperatures? (Chapter three) The "cool" daylight coming in the window will make your subject look blue if the camera has been adjusted for the "warm" light of the bulbs. For both these reasons you'll probably get best results by closing the curtains and using light bulbs only.

Lights bring light, but they also bring shadows, and shadows don't always look good on TV. Lots of large dark shadows look unnatural. And if you've ever held a flashlight under your chin and shone the light up onto your face, you'll know that shadows don't make people's faces look pleasing. Thus, in lighting your video production, you want to spread the light around in the room, pointing at your subjects from different angles. You should also put some light in back of your subjects to lighten the effect of the shadows there. If possible, have the actors stand far enough away from the walls so that their shadows don't show.

To soften shadows, some lights should also be *diffuse.* This means that they should spread light softly in all directions rather than pointing in one direction as a flashlight does. To make lights diffuse

3-POINT LIGHTING
OVERHEAD VIEW

Back light

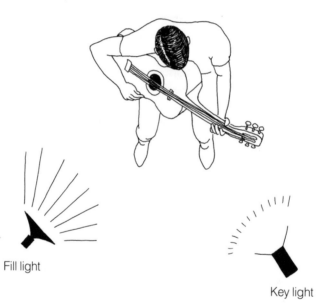

Fill light

Key light

(especially bare bulbs like you find in scoop lights), you can reflect lights off white walls and ceilings instead of aiming them directly at the subjects.

Professionals often use *three-point lighting* for their indoor shoots, and if you want to try something fancy, you can, too. Like the crew shooting the professional video in chapter two, you'd use a strong *key light* as the brightest light shining on the subjects. As you can see in the diagram on page 70, it should be mounted in front and slightly to the side of the subjects. A more diffuse *fill light,* mounted slightly to the other side, helps soften the shadows caused by the key light. A *backlight* fills in the shadows behind the subjects.

Once you've set up these basic lights, you can set up more lights to achieve the effect you want. Watch music video clips on TV to get an idea of what dramatic lighting can look like. You can even try using colored light bulbs for effect!

Outside, with the sunlight all around, it's not necessary to have any extra lights. However, you should be aware of what direction the light is coming from. As we said earlier, don't point your camera directly at the sun or you could burn out the tube. You should also avoid shooting toward the sun because it will make the subject appear too dark.

Before you shoot, especially if you're shooting indoors, try testing out your lighting in advance. You can do this either by shooting a sample tape and then playing it back on a VCR hooked up to a TV set, or, if you're shooting in a room with a TV set, keeping the VCR hooked up to the TV throughout the shoot. (See illustration on page 78.) Your TV set becomes a *monitor,* which can give the whole crew, not just the cameraperson with the little electronic viewfinder, an idea of what the video looks like as it's being made. This will help you spot problems with lighting, color, or awkward scenery before they become a permanent part of your video. If the cameraperson has the camera on a tripod, he or she can use the monitor rather than the viewfinder to compose the picture. Just make sure you turn the sound on the TV set all the way down. Otherwise, it will show up on your video's soundtrack if you're recording sound with your picture, and it will be distracting even if you're not.

REHEARSING THE CAST

When your scenery and lights are all set, then it's time to rehearse the cast. All cast members should be given a copy of the script in advance in order to study their parts. Even those with small parts should know what's going on before the day of the shoot.

With a performance video, since you shoot the whole video at once, you should rehearse it all at once. A conceptual video, on the other hand, should be rehearsed one scene at a time, with the rehearsal occurring right before each scene is shot. As the actors are rehearsing, following the director's directions as to where to stand, the cameraperson should rehearse his or her moves, too, practicing moving the camera when it's supposed to be moved and using the zoom when it's required by the script.

If you're shooting sound, too, then rehearsal is also time to do a sound check. The musicians should play a few bars, and the sound person should listen to the results through earphones connected to the camera's earphone jack. He or she should listen for problems with the sound system (buzzes, hums, hisses) and for sound quality—whether, for instance, one member of the band sounds too loud in comparison with the others, or whether the instruments are drowning out the singing. These situations can be corrected by either moving the mikes or asking people to sing or play louder or softer.

ACTION

When *everything*—scenery, lights, camera, and perhaps sound—is set up and you've run through one or two rehearsals that satisfy everyone, then it's time to shoot. The camera should start running right as the action starts. You don't want each scene to begin with a

Tina Turner adds excitement to her videos with strong singing and dancing.

few seconds showing your actors just standing around, especially if you're editing video in the camera and can't edit out this footage later. It may take many tries before you get a scene—or if you're doing a performance video, then the entire clip—right.

If you're shooting a conceptual video with many different scenes, every scene that's a possible take should be reviewed by the director. The scene can either be reviewed in the camera's electronic viewfinder or on a monitor. (If you're using neither, you won't be able to review scenes.) Any scene that's not satisfactory should be rewound to the end of the last scene and shot again. This is also part of editing in the camera. Making a tape by editing in the camera is like building a pile of blocks. If you suddenly notice that a block in the middle of the stack is imperfect, you can't replace it without undoing the rest of the blocks.

Even if you're not recording sound at the time you're shooting the video, sound is still important. Playing back an audio tape recording of your song while you shoot will help ensure that each scene is exactly the right length to fit the part of the song it goes along with. For example, if the script says a scene should start at the beginning of the guitar solo and finish when the singers start singing, that part of the song should be played while shooting that scene to guide the actors. The sound person should start the tape a few seconds before the solo. Then the cameraperson should start shooting and the actors acting exactly when the solo begins and stop when the singers start. If you use this technique, the finished video won't be any longer or shorter than the song is when you either finally transfer the music onto the video tape or when you play the sound with the finished film. (We explain how to transfer sound in the next chapter.)

Even though playing the music during the shoot can give you accurate results on how long the clip will be, it's not *that* accurate a technique. There may be a few seconds difference between the song and the action on the video, so don't make the scenes *too* short.

When you finally finish the last scene on your script (and, we warn you, it will take a lot longer than you think!), that's known as a "wrap"—you've completed the picture portion of your video clip.

7
POST PRODUCTION

You've finished shooting all the footage you need for your video. The sets are torn down, costumes put away, equipment back where it came. But you're not done yet. The last stage of putting together a video is "postproduction" (after production), in which you'll tie all the loose ends together.

How long the postproduction process takes will depend on how you've shot your video. For most professional video makers, most of postproduction is taken up with editing—picking the best scenes from all the footage that was shot during production and then rearranging them in the right order. You'll need to edit if you've shot the scenes to your video out of order, either on film or on video. If you've done a one-take performance video or a conceptual video that you edited in the camera, however, you can skip this process and move on to the final steps—adding sound if sound hasn't been recorded already and making copies of your video to pass around.

If you've used film, then step one before editing is to get the film *developed*. This costs about seven dollars or more per roll.

EDITING YOUR VIDEO

Film editing is "hands-on" editing. You actually touch the developed film, identifying the pictures and deciding whether you want them in the video by holding them up to the light. It's possible to edit with nothing but scissors and special editing tape, but it helps to have a few other tools. Some photo stores sell or rent home editing systems. These include miniature versions of the editing tables the professionals use, with a tiny screen to see the image and two spools to hold the film. Some also have a film cutter.

Try to use your script as a strict guide in editing. If you start moving scenes around in a way not described in the script, chances are you'll have a space somewhere in the song without any picture to fill it. If you shot the scenes in a different order from the order they were in the script, you should use your shooting schedule as a guide to where in your footage you might find each scene.

Cut out each strip of film you'd like to use in the final video. Then label each one for easy identification with a label made of masking tape, and hang them in order on a wall or a string stretched across the room. Now it's time to put the film back together, a process called *splicing*. Each spot where two pieces of film are joined together is called a *splice*. Use the special splicing tape you buy at a photo store and apply it very carefully to avoid hurting any of the pictures. Kodak makes prepackaged splicing tapes, called Presstapes, available in many stores. It's also very important to keep the film clean. Dirt, dust, and even fingerprints will show up on the screen. Hold each piece of film by the edges.

Unlike film, with video editing you can't actually see the picture by looking at the tape. (In fact, if you actually handled the tape, you'd probably do a lot of damage to it.) Because the video picture is magnetically encoded in the tape, the only way to see it is by playing that tape on a VCR, and watching it on TV. So, if you plan to do postproduction editing, you'll need two VCRs and one or two TV sets. You put the original tape—the one with everything you shot on it—into the first VCR and hook it up to a TV so that you can review everything you shot on the screen. In the second VCR, you put a blank tape. You'll transfer the scenes you want in the final video onto the blank tape, in the order you want them to go in, by recording a signal sent by the first VCR. Make sure the tape-speed selector on this VCR is set at the fastest speed, either SP or Beta II (or Beta I on some older Beta recorders). When you transfer a scene from one video cassette to another, it doesn't disappear from the first tape. You wind up with the same scene on two different cassettes. It's useful to have a second TV set hooked up to the second VCR. That way, you'll be able to review the results of your editing while you're doing it, and if you make some mistakes, you'll know about them, and can correct them, right away.

Before you start your video editing, review all the original footage by watching it on the original TV set. As you're watching, decide which scenes you want to use. Remember your decisions by writing them down on a piece of paper. (For example, write down that you liked the second version of the scene where everyone was dancing the best.) To keep track of where to find the best scenes in your footage, you could make a note of the number on the VCR's tape counter at the beginning of each of these scenes. Then, after you've played the tape all the way through, you can find each scene again by rewinding the tape until its number shows up on the tape counter. These tape counters are not absolutely accurate, but they'll get you within a few seconds of the point you want. Then you can find the exact beginning of the scene by looking at the TV set.

The two VCRs and the TV set or sets should be connected together as shown in the diagrams on page 78. A standard audio/video cable will run from the video *output jack* on the VCR with the original tape (because you want the signals to go *out* of that VCR) to the video *input jack* on the VCR with the blank tape.

When you're *transferring* a scene, you'll be playing the tape on the first VCR at the same time you'll be recording on the second VCR. But instead of starting the play and record action of the VCRs from the "stop" position, you'll start them from the "pause" position, using the VCR's *pause controls* (sometimes called "freeze frame").

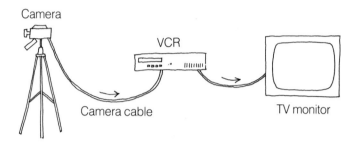

Camera

VCR

Camera cable

TV monitor

Hooking up a VCR, camera, and monitor. If you want to see a picture of what you are shooting on a TV monitor screen, connect a video cable from the output of your VCR to the video input of the TV monitor. The picture from the camera will appear on the TV screen whenever the camera is turned on. (If you use a conventional TV set instead of a monitor, connect it to the VCR with an RF cable.)

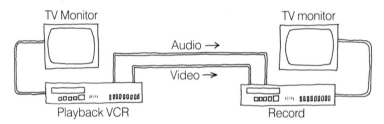

TV Monitor

TV monitor

Audio →

Video →

Playback VCR

Record

Hooking up two VCRs for dubbing. To transfer, or "dub," pictures and sound from one VCR to another requires just two cables. Connect the video output of the VCR that will play back to the video input of the VCR that will record the copy. Connect the audio output of the playback VCR to the audio input of the record VCR. (Stereo VCRs will need two audio cables.) Then at the same time press the play button on the playback VCR and the record button on the record VCR. This will let you copy the pictures and sound from the tape in the playback VCR to a blank tape in the record VCR. You can hook up a TV set to each VCR (using the RF cable) to watch the scenes you want to transfer.

For the first VCR, you'll play the tape until it gets to the very beginning of a scene you want to record. Then you'll hit the pause button. Depending on your VCR, you'll see either a still picture or a blank screen on your TV set. For the second VCR, you'll play the tape until it gets to the place where you want the scene to start. Then you'll press pause. To start the first VCR playing again, you'll press the pause button again. To start the second VCR recording, you'll press the "record" button. (Some VCRs may work a little differently. Check your owner's manual before you start.) The key to editing, however, is to start playing the first VCR and recording on the second *at the exact same time*. One person could hit both buttons at the same time, or, if the VCRs are too far apart, two people could each hit one after one person says, "One, two, three, go."

To make editing a little easier, some people use a piece of equipment called an *editing controller*. Sometimes available for rental at video equipment stores, a controller works like an extra pair of hands: it turns on and off both VCRs at once. However, most controllers can only be used with two VCRs of the same brand.

Fortunately, with video editing, it's possible to repair your mistakes. If you stop a scene too soon, simply rewind both tapes and try the whole scene again. If you stop one too late, simply rewind the second VCR to the desired point (you'll need a second TV hooked up to the second VCR for this or possibly a TV that can take signals from two VCRs) and record over the last bit of that scene.

With either film or video editing, if you timed each scene to the song when you were shooting it and followed your script closely when editing, you'll probably come out with a video that plays in time with the song. If you want to be sure, you can always bring along your tape recorder (and perhaps your sound person) to the editing session. When you're reviewing the footage, time each scene to the part of the song it matches and note exactly by writing down what's happening on screen at the moments when that particular scene should begin and end. (You can't do this with film, unless you have a projector handy.)

As we noted earlier, editing with video is a tedious and inexact process. In many edits from one scene to another, you'll see a horizontal black bar rolling up the screen. This comes from two VCRs trying to match up their pictures. You may have seen a bar like this on a TV set in which the "vertical hold" control is not adjusted correctly.

When the picture part of your video is finally in order, whether you've edited in the camera or in postproduction, then it's time to transfer sound. (This step is for video users only.) As we explained in chapter three, video and audio are recorded in separate tracks on a video tape (except for hi-fi sound). Thus, you can add or replace audio on a video tape without disrupting the video at all.

This is exactly what you'll be doing when you add the sound. To do this, you should follow the instructions in your VCR's owner's manual for *audio dubbing*. (Remember, "dub" comes from "double" and means "to copy.") The process involves connecting the audio input jack (or jacks if your VCR records in stereo on the normal audio track) to the audio output on your tape recorder or stereo system. (Even if you've been using a portable tape recorder throughout production and postproduction, try to use a better-quality, nonportable tape recorder, or even a record player, hooked up to a stereo system for audio dubbing. This will give you better sound on the final tape.) You then wind the tapes to the beginning of the video and the beginning of the song. Push the pause button on your VCR, then push the audio dub and play buttons at the same time. Hit the pause button next and hit the play button on your tape recorder (or start the record) at the same time. When the song has finished playing, you'll have a video tape with picture and sound.

You may not get the "synch" you want between video and audio at the first try. No problem! Simply rewind both tapes and try again. You can even see the results of what you're taping by hooking up your VCR to a TV and your audio source to a speaker (if one's not built in already). Thus, you'll be able to see problems without waiting for the whole song to be recorded.

DISTRIBUTING YOUR VIDEO

Congratulations! Whether it's in video or film form, you've got a completed music video. If it's in video, you can make copies of it to give all your friends whose families have VCRs. To make a copy, you need two VCRs, one for your completed tape and one for the blank tape you're going to fill with pictures and music. As in the diagram on page 78, connect the two VCRs with cables by attaching the video output jack of VCR number one to the video input of VCR number two and the audio output jack of number one to the audio input of number two. (If both VCRs are stereo, connect the left and right channel audio outputs and inputs separately. If only one is stereo, connect the audio jack of one to the two audio jacks of the other with a "Y" connector cable.) Turn on VCR number two to record and VCR number one to play. When number one has finished playing through your video, you'll have a second copy of the tape. The two VCRs you connect don't have to be in the same format. Connect VCRs of different formats in the same way.

You may notice that the copies you make don't look or sound quite as good as the original. This is because some picture and sound quality gets lost during dubbing. To be sure that your copies have the best quality possible, always copy them from your original video—don't use a dub to make another dub.

If you want to be sure you'll never record over your video accidentally while you're trying to play it, there's something called a *safety tab* on the back of each VHS and Beta cassette. Simply push in that little tab, using a pencil or pen, and you won't be able to record any more on that cassette. You'll only be able to play it. The 8-mm video cassettes have a tiny safety switch that you can move from record-and-play to play-only.

If you find you like making music videos and think you're good at it, maybe there's a future for you in video or film. There are many jobs in the field. Some require technical know-how, others creativity, and many require both.

In the meantime, there are a number of things you can do with your videos besides show them to friends and family. You can look into showing them at your school, at the local Y, or to any youth group you belong to. Many organizations today have equipment for showing video tapes. Just make sure that your cassette is in the right format to play back on their equipment.

It you think your video is good enough, you can try entering it in a contest or even getting it played on a local TV station. If you used a professional song for your video, however, you can't do either unless you get permission from the record company to use it.

There is at least one nationwide contest for video enthusiasts: the Sony/American Film Institute contest, which in its first year, 1984, was won by a high school student. For information and entry blanks, write to Video Contest, P.O. Box 200, Hollywood, CA 90078.

Depending on your local TV stations, you might even be able to get your video on TV. Look for the stations based in smaller cities near you. Do any of them have a video clip show? Is it produced locally? Do they ever play amateur video clips? If so, find out the procedures for submitting a clip by writing or calling the station, and then send yours in.

Local cable stations are probably an even better opportunity for getting your video on TV. Many local cable systems have public access channels—channels for which the general public (that's you!) can produce TV shows. Find out about this channel from your cable company. Ask who's in charge of it and how someone goes about getting a program on. Since videos are so short, maybe a talk show host of a regular show on the channel would be interested in giving your video a whirl.

But the excitement of seeing your ideas take shape on the screen is worth all the work even if you only show your video to a few of your friends. And, whether this is the first of many music videos for you or only a one-time experiment in the medium, you are now a real insider in the world of music video.

GLOSSARY

ASA—A rating describing how sensitive film is to light. ASA ratings in home movie film range from 40 to 200. Also called *ISO*.

assistant camera—The person who helps the *cameraperson* do his or her job by carrying equipment, changing film or video tape, and, sometimes, focusing.

audio cassette—A *cassette* containing *audio tape*.

audio dubbing—Transferring an audio soundtrack from a record or audio tape to the soundtrack of a video tape.

audio tape—Plastic tape covered with metal particles and used to record sound. Usually comes in an *audio cassette*.

audio tape recorder—A device that records sound on *audio tape* and plays that sound back.

auto-focus—A feature found on many video cameras. Auto-focus cameras focus themselves by judging the distance from the camera to the subject.

backlight—The light or lights set up in back of the actors on a *set*. This helps prevent shadows from showing up in the video.

backlight compensation—A video camera feature used when the subject has bright light, such as light from a window, in back of him or her. Using the backlight compensation switch prevents the subject's face from looking dark in comparison.

Beta—One of the four home video *formats*. There are Beta *video tapes*, Beta *VCRs*, and Beta *camcorders*. Beta tapes can only be played on VCRs and camcorders of the same format.

brightness switch—Found on home film cameras, this switch is adjusted to let the correct amount of light into the camera.

broadcast TV—The type of television reception in which channels are received through a TV antenna. Some broadcast channels also go to some homes through a cable, as *cable TV* channels do.

cable TV—The type of television reception in which channels come to your home through a cable.

camcorder—A piece of video equipment that combines the functions of a *portable VCR* and a *video camera*. The simplest equipment to use for home video movies.

camera angle—Refers to the relationship between the camera's position and the subject's position. This determines what the picture you're shooting will look like. For example, a picture shot when the camera is far away and to the right of the subject will look very different from one shot when the camera is close up to and right in front of the subject.

cameraperson—The person on a music video shoot (or any home movie shoot) who is in charge of operating and taking care of the camera.

cassette—A small plastic box containing *video tape* or *audio tape* wrapped around two spools. The tape always stays in the cassette. The cassette should never be opened.

character generator—Found on some fancy *video cameras*, a character generator puts letters and numbers onto the video picture for making titles.

choreograph—To plan out where on the stage or *set* the actors should be moving during a scene.

close-up shot—A camera angle. Close-up shots show a person from the bottom of the neck to the top of the head.

color balance—The relationship, or balance, between the different *color temperatures* in a video picture.

color balance controls—These enable a video camera to adjust to the various *color temperatures* of light. They include *color temperature controls* and *white balance controls.*

color temperature—Not to be confused with the kind of temperature we mean when we talk about the weather, color temperature refers to a quality of light. Red light is "warm," and blue light is "cold."

color temperature control—A switch on a video camera for *color temperature* adjustments. It usually has positions for outside light, incandescent (yellowish, indoor) light, and fluorescent (bluish, indoor) light.

conceptual video—A video clip based on an idea or a story, with people acting like fictional characters rather than being themselves playing music, as in a *performance video.*

defocus shot—A shot used to make a transition from one scene to another. This is done by purposely making the very end of the first scene blurry.

developing—The process of using chemicals to turn exposed film (film you've used in a camera) into film you can play back with a projector. Usually done by professionals.

diffuse—Referring to lighting, diffuse describes light that spreads softly in all directions instead of being pointed in a narrow beam like a flashlight's light.

director—The person in charge of the creative aspects of a music video shoot, who decides, for example, where the camera should be set up, how the lights should be arranged, where the actors should stand and how they should move, and so on.

dolly shot—A type of shot in which the camera actually moves. You can use a dolly shot, for example, to follow an actor down the sidewalk. You can do this by putting the camera and the cameraperson on a wagon or on almost anything that rolls.

dub—The process of taking material on one *video cassette* or *audio cassette* and putting it on another. "Dub" comes from "double." See *transfer*. "Dub" also refers to the second video or audio cassette, the one with the dubbed material on it.

edit—To take the film or video footage you've shot and select from it only the scenes you want in your final video, then put them into the order in which you want them to appear. With film, you can edit by cutting up and taping back together the developed film. With video, you have to *dub* the scenes you want to keep onto a second *video cassette,* in the right order.

editing controller—A piece of equipment that makes editing with video a little easier. It controls two *VCRs* of the same brand so that you can start and stop them at the same time.

editing in the camera—You can edit while making a clip with video equipment by using this technique. If you don't like a scene you've just recorded, you rewind the tape to where the scene began and record over it.

8-mm film (eight-millimeter film)—*Film* that is 8 mm (about .3 inch) wide. It can only be used with 8-mm film cameras, not with *Super 8* cameras.

8-mm video—One of the four home video *formats,* using very small *cassettes* and *video tape* only 8 mm (about .3 inch) wide. Eight-mm video cassettes can only be used with 8-mm VCRs and 8-mm camcorders.

electronic viewfinder—Found on some *video cameras* and *camcorders,* an electronic viewfinder (sometimes called "EVF") is a tiny, usually black-and-white TV screen. The cameraperson looks at it to see what he or she is recording.

establishing shot—Always a *wide shot,* an establishing shot is the shot at the beginning of a scene that lets the viewer see the whole room or area where the action is about to take place.

external microphones—*Microphones* that are not the microphones that come with a *video camera.* You can plug these into most video cameras in order to get better sound for a *performance video.*

extra—A person with a small part in a video clip. Extras are usually found in the background, for example, walking down the street where the stars of the video are standing.

extra high grade (EHG)—The best-quality *video tape*. Sometimes called *super high grade*.

extreme close-up—A camera angle. In an extreme close-up, the picture shows less than a person's face, usually just the eyes, nose, and mouth, not the forehead or the hair.

fade-in and fade-out—Used to make a transition from one scene to the next. In fade-in, the screen starts blank and the picture gradually appears. In fade-out, the picture gradually turns into a blank screen.

fill light—A soft light (unlike a spotlight) used to lighten up dark corners on the set.

film—A material coated with chemicals that respond to light and thus can make pictures. "Film" can also refer to a movie made with film and to the whole process of making a movie with film.

film camera—A camera designed to expose film to light. In a film movie camera, a long strip of film runs past an opening letting light into the camera.

focus—To adjust the *lens* on a *film camera*, *video camera*, or *camcorder* so that the pictures it is making will be clear, not blurry.

format—Refers to methods of making pictures with video or film equipment. There are four formats in home video—*VHS*, *VHS-C*, *Beta*, and *8 mm*. They all use different-size *cassettes*. In home movie film, there are two formats—*8 mm* and *Super 8*.

frame—One of the thousands of individual pictures that make up a video or film movie. Video movies show the viewer thirty frames a second. Film movies show twenty-four frames a second.

gaffer—The person on a shoot who is in charge of setting up the lights.

Hi-Fi—Short for high fidelity; a method of recording very high quality sound on a *video tape*. Hi-Fi VCRs record a Hi-Fi *soundtrack* and a normal audio soundtrack. The Hi-Fi soundtrack can be used only for performance videos, not for conceptual videos, where the sound is added later.

high grade—Refers to *video tape* quality. Better than *standard grade,* but not as good as *extra high grade* or *super high grade.*

input jack—A small hole on a *VCR,* an *audio tape recorder,* or other equipment into which you plug in a cable bringing picture and/or sound information from another piece of equipment.

iris—On a camera, the opening that lets in light to the part of the camera that makes the picture. Most *video cameras* and *film cameras* have irises that adjust themselves automatically to the amount of light that's coming in.

key light—The brightest light on a set. It's used to light up the subjects in the picture, usually shining on their faces. Like a spotlight.

L-500—Video tape in the *Beta* format. L-500 is the length of tape that will play for two hours in the Beta II speed.

lens—The part of a video camera or film camera that lets in light and focuses it to make a sharp picture.

lip-synching—When a performer in a music video pretends to be singing but is only mouthing the words to an already recorded song, he or she is lip-synching.

long-form video—A music video that lasts longer than a regular song. It may contain several songs or just one song and lots of talking.

lux—A measure of brightness. Video cameras are rated in lux to tell you how much light you need to make good pictures. A camera rated at less than 30 lux usually needs only normal room light to make good pictures.

macro—A setting on some camera lenses that allows you to focus on objects very close to the camera.

ME—Metal evaporated. A kind of 8-mm video tape. Use this kind if it's recommended in your 8-mm camcorder or 8-mm VCR owner's manual.

medium shot—A camera angle that shows a person from about the waist up.

microphone—A microphone is used to record sound on video tape, audio tape, or sound film. It can either be built into the camera or be a separate *external microphone.*

minimum illumination—The smallest amount of light a camera needs to make good pictures. It is usually measured in *lux*.

monitor—A TV set used during a video shoot to watch the picture as it's being recorded. It's connected either to a *VCR* or a *camcorder*.

MP—Metal particle. A kind of 8-mm video tape. Use this kind if it's recommended in your 8-mm camcorder or 8-mm VCR owner's manual.

MTV—Music Television. A cable TV channel that shows music video clips twenty-four hours a day.

multipin connector—A plug with many little pins. These are found on either end of the cord used to connect a camera and a VCR. Some cameras and VCRs use ten-pin connectors and some use fourteen-pin connectors. You should make sure you have the right connectors when you rent video equipment.

output jack—A small hole on a *VCR, audio tape recorder*, or other equipment into which you plug in a cable that takes picture and/or sound information to another piece of equipment.

pan—A shot in which a camera moves horizontally from right to left or left to right.

pause control—A control found on most VCRs that temporarily stops the video tape from playing so that it can start up again very quickly. Many VCRs show a still, or freeze frame, picture on the TV screen when the "pause" button is pushed.

performance video—A video clip shot while the band was actually performing the song.

pickup tube—In most video cameras, the pickup tube is the part that turns the light focused by the lens into a picture. Because these tubes are very sensitive to light, a video camera should never be pointed at the sun or a bright light.

picture element—One of the thousands of tiny dots that make up a video picture.

portable VCR—A VCR for shooting video, small enough to be carried around. Most come in two parts: a *tuner/timer*, which stays at home, and a recorder, which goes on a shoot and runs on a *rechargeable battery*.

postproduction—The phase of making a video that occurs after the *shoot* is over. It can include *editing, audio dubbing,* and making copies of the video.

preproduction—The phase of making a video that occurs before the *shoot.* It can include drawing a *storyboard,* writing a *script,* making costumes, and preparing the *sets.*

producer—The person responsible for making all the arrangements for a video. His or her responsibilities usually include getting permission to use the different locations, renting equipment, and making sure everyone else knows what they are supposed to do.

production—The actual shooting of a video clip.

production assistant—Someone who helps set up and shoot a video. PAs, as they're sometimes called, build the sets, help carry equipment, and pitch in whenever else they're needed.

reaction shot—A close-up shot that shows a person's reaction to something else that happens in the video.

rechargeable battery—A battery that can be used over and over again. It is recharged with electricity from a wall socket.

record/review—A feature on some video cameras that allows you to see the last few seconds of a scene you've just shot in the camera's *electronic viewfinder.*

roll—A moving horizontal line that sometimes appears on a TV screen in a video movie when two different scenes are edited together.

safety tab—A small tab on the back of a video cassette that, when pushed, allows the tape to be played only, not recorded on.

scanning—The process used by a TV set to make a picture. The TV creates a picture one *picture element* at a time, scanning along horizontal lines from the top of the screen to the bottom.

script—The written description of what will happen in a music video. It includes the words to the song, the actions of the actors, and the *camera angles.*

set—The background for a scene in a video. Also, the place where a scene in a video is shot.

shoot—The phase of making a music video when the actual taping or filming is being done. Also, the act of taping or filming with a camera.

shot—A small part of a music video made without stopping the camera.

sound person—The person on a video shoot responsible for the sound. In a *performance video,* he or she sets up the microphones and makes sure the sound is recorded properly. In a *conceptual video,* he or she plays back the song, matching each part of the song with the scene being shot.

soundtrack—The sound that accompanies a music video.

splice—To connect two pieces of film using a small piece of special tape, known as splicing tape. Also, the part of the film where two pieces have been spliced together.

standard grade—Ordinary-quality video tape, normally the least expensive.

storyboard—A series of pictures, like a comic strip, illustrating what will happen in a music video.

subject—The person or thing that's being taped or filmed with a camera.

Super 8 film—A type of home movie film that is 8-mm (about .3 inch) wide. It has a slightly larger picture than *8-mm film* and can be used only with a Super 8 home movie camera.

super high grade (SHG)—The best-quality video tape. Sometimes called *extra high grade.*

synchronous—At the same time.

T-120—Video tape in the *VHS* format. T-120 is the length of tape that will play for two hours in the standard-play (SP) mode.

tabletop VCR—A *video cassette recorder* designed to sit on a table or shelf.

talkie—A film movie with a *soundtrack.* Before the first talkie movie came out in 1927, movies were silent.

tape—An abbreviation of *video tape* or *audio tape.*

TC-20—Video tape in the *VHS-C* format. A TC-20 tape plays for twenty minutes in the SP mode.

telephoto—The effect of a lens that magnifies the picture so that objects in the distance seem closer. The opposite of *wide angle.*

three-point lighting—Using three different lights—a *key light,* a *fill light,* and a *backlight*—to light a *set.*

transfer—The process of copying pictures and sound from one video cassette to another or from film to video tape.

tripod—A three-legged stand for a camera.

TTL viewfinder—Found on some video cameras and many film cameras, a "through-the-lens" viewfinder lets the cameraperson see what the camera is aimed at.

tuner/timer—The part of many portable VCRs that stays home when you're shooting. It's used to receive TV programs for recording.

unidirectional mike—A microphone designed to pick up sounds coming from only the direction in which it is aimed.

VCR—An abbreviation for *video cassette recorder.*

VHS—One of the four home video *formats.* There are VHS *video tapes,* VHS *VCRs,* and VHS *camcorders.* VHS tapes can only be played on VCRs and camcorders of the same format.

VHS-C—Another video *format.* This format is used mainly for making video movies. Thus, there are VHS-C *portable VCRs* and VHS-C *camcorders,* but no VHS-C *tabletop VCRs.* VHS-C can be played on VHS-C equipment and on VHS equipment if you use a special adapter.

video—A method of recording moving pictures that uses electrical impulses.

video camera—An instrument that changes light entering through its *lens* into electrical impulses. In order to record video, a video camera must be connected to a *video cassette recorder.*

video cassette—A *cassette* containing *video tape.*

video cassette recorder—A piece of equipment that records moving pictures on a *video cassette* and plays those pictures back. Video cassette recorders (VCRs) can be portable or tabletop.

video disc player—Like a record player, only it plays pictures and sound.

video facility—A place where *postproduction* work is done on professional music videos. Video facilities have equipment for *editing* and *dubbing*.

video signal—A stream of bursts of electricity that makes a video picture. A video signal can travel by cables between a *VCR* and a TV set, or between two VCRs.

video tape—Plastic tape covered with metal particles and used to record pictures and sound. Usually comes in a *video cassette.*

viewfinder—The place on a camera where you look to see the picture the camera is seeing. In video, there are *electronic viewfinders* and *TTL* (through-the-lens) *viewfinders*. In film, there are TTL viewfinders and viewfinders that don't look through the lens.

viewfinder indications—Letters and lights seen in most video camera viewfinders and some film camera viewfinders that let you know about the camera's operations. Indications tell you, for example, when you are recording, whether you have enough light, and whether you have enough battery power.

white balance—A control, found on many video cameras, that must be set before each scene is shot to make colors turn out right. You set white balance by aiming the camera at a white surface and pushing the white balance button for a few seconds.

wide angle—The effect of a lens that makes objects near the camera seem farther away. A wide-angle effect also enables you to record a wider view of the scene in front of the camera. The opposite of *telephoto.*

wide shot—A camera angle. Wide shots show the whole scene: the people from head to toe and their surroundings.

zoom—A control on video and film cameras that moves the camera's lens from *wide-angle* to *telephoto* settings.

FOR FURTHER READING

Costello, Marjorie, and Heiss, Michael. *How to Select and Use Home Video Equipment.* Tucson: HP Books, 1984. Informative explanations of equipment.

Hirschman, Robert, and Procter, Richard. *How to Shoot Better Video.* Milwaukee: Hal Leonard Publishing, 1985. Thorough, up-to-date guide to making home video movies.

Langman, Larry. *The Video Encyclopedia.* New York: Garland Publishing, 1983. Technical explanations of video terms.

Levine, Pamela; Glasser, Jeffrey; and Gach, Stephen. *The Complete Guide to Home Video Production.* New York: Holt, Rinehart and Winston, 1984. Excellent step-by-step how-to guide.

Porter, Martin. *Making Video Movies.* New York: Simon & Schuster, 1984. Good guide to video movie shooting.

Shore, Michael. *The Rolling Stone Book of Rock Video.* New York: Rolling Stone Press, 1984. Comprehensive, exhaustive history of music video.

INDEX